PORTFOLIO / PENGUIN

ALL MARKETERS ARE LIARS

SETH GODIN is the author of *Tribes*, *The Dip*, *Purple Cow*, *Permission Marketing*, and other international bestsellers that have changed the way business people think and act. He's the most influential business blogger in the world and consistently one of the twenty-five most widely read bloggers in the English language. He's also the founder and CEO of Squidoo.com and a very popular speaker. He lives in Westchester, New York.

D0038364

ALL MARKETERS ARE LIARS

THE UNDERGROUND CLASSIC
THAT EXPLAINS HOW MARKETING
REALLY WORKS—AND WHY
AUTHENTICITY IS THE BEST
MARKETING OF ALL

Seth Godin

PORTFOLIO/PENGUIN

PORTFOLIO/PENGUIN
Published by the Penguin Group
Penguin Group (USA) Inc., 375 Hudson Street,
New York, New York 10014, U.S.A.
Penguin Group (Canada), 90 Eglinton Avenue East, Suite 700,
Toronto, Ontario, Canada M4P 2Y3
(a division of Pearson Penguin Canada Inc.)
Penguin Books Ltd, 80 Strand, London WC2R 0RL, England
Penguin Ireland, 25 St. Stephen's Green, Dublin 2, Ireland
(a division of Penguin Books Ltd)
Penguin Books Australia Ltd, 250 Camberwell Road, Camberwell,
Victoria 3124, Australia
(a division of Pearson Australia Group Pty Ltd)
Penguin Books India Pvt Ltd, 11 Community Centre, Panchsheel Park,
New Delhi – 110 017, India
Penguin Group (NZ), 67 Apollo Drive, Rosedale, Auckland 0632,
New Zealand (a division of Pearson New Zealand Ltd)
Penguin Books (South Africa) (Pty) Ltd, 24 Sturdee Avenue,
Rosebank, Johannesburg 2196, South Africa

Penguin Books Ltd, Registered Offices:
80 Strand, London WC2R 0RL, England

First published in the United States of America by Portfolio, a member of Penguin Group (USA) Inc. 2009
This paperback edition published 2012

7   9   10   8

THE LIBRARY OF CONGRESS HAS CATALOGED THE HARDCOVER EDITION AS FOLLOWS:

ISBN 978-1-59184-303-0 (hc.)
ISBN 978-1-59184-533-1 (pbk.)
CIP data available

Printed in the United States of America

Don't just tell me the facts,
tell me a story instead.

Be remarkable!
Be consistent!
Be authentic!

Tell your story to people who are inclined to believe it.

Marketing is powerful. Use it wisely.

Live the lie.

CONTENTS

STEP 2: PEOPLE NOTICE ONLY THE NEW AND THEN MAKE A GUESS 75

STEP 3: FIRST IMPRESSIONS START THE STORY

STEP 4: GREAT MARKETERS TELL STORIES WE BELIEVE

EXAMPLES: STORIES FRAMED AROUND WORLDVIEWS

IMPORTANT ASIDE: FIBS AND FRAUDS

STEP 5: MARKETERS WITH AUTHENTICITY THRIVE

PREFACE

You believe things that aren't true.

Let me say that a different way: Many things that are true are true because you believe them.

The ideas in this book have elected a president, grown nonprofit causes, created billionaires, and fueled movements. They've also led to great jobs, fun dates, and more than a few interactions that mattered.

I've seen this book in campaign headquarters and carried around at evangelical conferences. I've also gotten e-mail from people who have used it in Japan and the UK and yes, Akron, Ohio. The ideas here work because they are simple tools to understand what human beings do when they encounter you and your organization.

Here's the first half of the simple summary: We believe what we want to believe, and once we believe something, it becomes a self-fulfilling truth. (Jump ahead a few paragraphs to read the critical second part of this summary)

If you think that more expensive wine is better, then it is. If you think your new boss is going to be more effective, then she will be.

If you love the way a car handles, then you're going to enjoy driving it.

That sounds so obvious, but if it is, why is it so ignored? Ignored by marketers, ignored by ordinarily rational consumers, and ignored by our leaders.

Once we move beyond the simple satisfaction of needs, we move into the complex satisfaction of wants. And wants are hard to measure and difficult to understand. Which makes marketing the fascinating exercise it is.

Here's the second part of the summary: When you are busy telling stories to people who want to hear them, you'll be tempted to tell stories that just don't hold up. Lies. Deceptions.

This sort of storytelling used to work pretty well. Joe McCarthy became famous while lying about the "Communist threat." Bottled water companies made billions while lying about the purity of their product compared with tap water in the developed world.

The thing is, lying doesn't pay off anymore. That's because when you fabricate a story that just doesn't hold up to scrutiny, you get caught. Fast.

So, it's tempting to put up a demagogue for vice president, but it doesn't take long for the reality to catch up with the story. It's tempting to spin a tall tale about a piece of technology or a customer service policy, but once we see it in the wild, we talk about it and you wither away.

That's why I think this book is one of the most important I've written. It talks about two sides of a universal truth, one that has built every successful brand, organization, and candidate, and one that we rarely have the words to describe.

Here are the questions I hope you'll ask (your boss, your colleagues, your clients) after you've read this book:

"What's your story?"

"Will the people who need to hear this story believe it?"

"Is it true?"

Every day, we see mammoth technology brands fail because they neglected to ask and answer these questions. We see worthy candidates gain little attention and flawed ones bite the dust. There are small businesses that are so focused on what they do that they forget to take the time to describe the story of why they do it. And on and on.

If what you're doing matters, really matters, then I hope you'll take the time to tell a story. A story that resonates and a story that can become true.

The irony is that I did a lousy job of telling a story about this book. The original jacket seemed to be about lying and seemed to imply that my readers (marketers) were bad people. For people who bothered to read the book, they could see that this wasn't true, but by the time they opened the book, it was too late. A story was already told.

I had failed.

You don't get a second chance in publishing very often, and I'm thrilled that my publisher let me try a new jacket, and triply thrilled that it worked. After all, you're reading this.

So, go tell a story. If it doesn't resonate, tell a different one.

When you find a story that works, live that story, make it true, authentic, and subject to scrutiny. All marketers are storytellers. Only the losers are liars.

ALL
MARKETERS
ARE LIARS

HIGHLIGHTS

I have no intention of telling you the truth.

Instead I'm going to tell you a story. This is a story about why marketers must forsake any attempt to communicate nothing but the facts, and must instead focus on what people believe and then work to tell them stories that add to their worldview.

Make no mistake. This is not about tactics or spin or little things that *might* matter. This is a whole new way of doing business. It's a fundamental shift in the paradigm of how ideas spread. **Either you're going to tell stories that spread, or you will become irrelevant.**

In the first few pages, I'll explain what the whole book is about, and then we'll take it apart, bit by bit, from the beginning, so you can learn how to tell stories too.

IN THE BEGINNING, THERE WAS THE STORY

Before marketing, before shopping carts and long before infomercials, people started telling themselves stories.

We noticed things. We noticed that the sun rose every morning and we invented a story about Helios and his chariot. People got sick and we made up stories about humors and bloodletting and we sent them to the barber to get well.

Stories make it easier to understand the world. Stories are the only way we know to spread an idea.

Marketers didn't invent storytelling. They just perfected it.

YOU'RE A LIAR

So am I.

Everyone is a liar. We tell ourselves stories because we're superstitious. Stories are shortcuts we use because we're too overwhelmed by data to discover all the details. The stories we tell ourselves are lies that make it far easier to live in a very complicated world. We tell stories about products, services, friends, job seekers, the New York Yankees and sometimes even the weather.

We tell ourselves stories that can't possibly be true, but believing those stories allows us to function. We know we're not telling ourselves the whole truth, but it works, so we embrace it.

We tell stories to our spouses, our friends, our bosses, our employees and our customers. Most of all, we tell stories to ourselves.

Marketers are a special kind of liar. Marketers lie to consumers because consumers demand it. Marketers tell the stories, and consumers believe them. Some marketers do it well. Others are pretty bad at it. Sometimes the stories help people get more done, enjoy life more and even live longer. Other times, when the story isn't authentic, it can have significant side effects and consumers pay the price.

The reason all successful marketers tell stories is that consumers insist on it. Consumers are used to telling stories to themselves and telling stories to each other, and it's just natural to buy stuff from someone who's telling us a story. People can't handle the truth.

GEORG RIEDEL IS A LIAR

Georg is a tenth-generation glassblower, an artisan pursuing an age-old craft. I'm told he's a very nice guy. And he's very good at telling stories.

His company makes wine glasses (and scotch glasses, whiskey glasses, espresso glasses and even water glasses). He and his staff fervently believe that there is a perfect (and different) shape for every beverage.

According to Riedel's Web site: "The delivery of a wine's 'message,' its bouquet and taste, depends on the form of the glass. It is the responsibility of a glass to convey the wine's messages in the best manner to the human senses."

Thomas Matthews, the executive editor of *Wine Spectator* magazine, said, "Everybody who ventures into a Riedel tasting starts as a skeptic. I did."

The skepticism doesn't last long. Robert Parker, Jr., the king of wine reviewers, said, "The finest glasses for both technical and hedonistic purposes are those made by Riedel. The effect of these glasses on fine wine is profound. I cannot emphasize enough what a difference they make."

Parker and Matthews and hundreds of other wine luminaries are now believers (and as a result, they are Riedel's best word-of-mouth marketers). Millions of wine drinkers around the world have been persuaded that a $200 bottle of wine (or a cheap bottle of Two-Buck Chuck) tastes better when served in the proper Riedel glass.

Tests done in Europe and the United States have shown that wine experts have no trouble discovering just how much better wine tastes in the correct glass. Presented with the same wine in both an ordinary kitchen glass and the proper Riedel glass, they rarely fail to find that the expensive glass delivers a far better experience.

This is a breakthrough. A $5 or a $20 or a $500 bottle of wine can be radically improved by using a relatively inexpensive (and reusable!) wine glass.

And yet when the *proper* tests are done *scientifically*— double-blind tests that eliminate any chance that the subject would know the shape of the glass—there is absolutely zero detectible difference between glasses. A $1 glass and a $20 glass deliver *precisely* the same impact on the wine: none.

So what's going on? Why do wine experts insist that the wine tastes better in a Riedel glass at the same time that scientists can easily prove it doesn't? The flaw in the experiment, as outlined by Daniel Zwerdling in *Gourmet* magazine, is that the reason the wine tastes better is that *people believe it should.* This makes sense, of course. Taste is subjective. If you think the pancakes at the IHOP taste better, then they do. Because you want them to.

Riedel sells millions of dollars' worth of glasses every year. He sells glasses to intelligent, well-off wine lovers who then proceed to enjoy their wine more than they did before.

Marketing, apparently, makes wine taste better.

Marketing, in the form of an expensive glass and the story that goes with it, has more impact on the taste of wine than oak casks or fancy corks or the rain in June. Georg Riedel makes your wine taste better by telling you a story.

SOME OF MY BEST FRIENDS ARE LIARS

Arthur Riolo is a world-class storyteller. Arthur sells real estate in my little town north of New York City. He sells a lot of real estate—more than all his competitors combined. That's because Arthur doesn't *sell* anything.

Anyone can tell you the specs of a house or talk to you about the taxes. But he doesn't. Instead, Arthur does something very different. He takes you and your spouse for a drive. You drive up and down the hills of a neighborhood as he points out house after house (houses that aren't for sale). He tells you who lives in that house and what they do and how they found the house and the name of their dog and what their kids are up to and how much they paid. He tells you a story about the different issues in town, the long-simmering rivalries between neighborhoods and the evolution and imminent demise of the Mother's Club. Then, and only then, does Arthur show you a house.

It might be because of Arthur's antique pickup truck or the fact that everyone in town knows him or the obvious pleasure he gets from the community, but sooner or later, you'll buy a house from Arthur. And not just because it's a good house. Because it's a good story.

Bonnie Siegler and Emily Obermann tell stories too. They are graphic designers in the toughest market in the world—New York City. And they claim their success is accidental. Bonnie and Emily run Number 17, a firm with clients like NBC, *Sex and the City* and the Mercer Hotel.

Everything about their firm, their site, their people, their office and their personalities tells a story. It's the same story; it's consistent. It's a story about two very funny and charismatic women who do iconoclastic work that's not for everyone. Their Web site is exactly one page long and some people think it has a typo on it. Their office is hidden behind a nondescript door in a nondescript building on an oddball corner of New York, but once the door opens, visitors are overwhelmed by fun, nostalgia, quirkiness and raw energy.

Nobody buys pure design from Number 17. They buy the way the process makes them feel.

So what do real estate, graphic design and wine glasses have in common? Not a lot. Not price point or frequency of purchase or advertising channels or even consumer sales. The only thing they have in common is that no one buys facts. They buy a story.

WANTS AND NEEDS

Does it really matter that the $80,000 Porsche Cayenne and the $36,000 VW Touareg are virtually the same vehicle, made in the same factory? Or that your new laptop is not measurably faster in actual use than the one it replaced? Why do consumers pay extra for eggs marketed as being antibiotic free—when *all* egg-laying chickens are raised without antibiotics, even the kind of chickens that lay cheap eggs?

The facts are irrelevant. In the short run, it doesn't matter one bit whether something is actually better or faster or more efficient. What matters is what the consumer believes.

A long time ago, there was money to be made in selling people a commodity. Making your product or service better and cheaper was a sure path to growth and profitability. Today, of course, the rules are different. Plenty of people can make something cheaper than you can, and offering a product or service that is measurably better for the same money is a hard edge to sustain.

Marketers profit because consumers buy what they want, not what they need. Needs are practical and objective, wants are irrational and subjective. And no matter what you sell—and whether you sell it to businesses or consumers—the path to profitable growth is in satisfying wants, not needs. (Of course, your product must really satisfy those wants, not just pretend to!)

CAN PUMAS REALLY CHANGE
YOUR LIFE?

In the coming pages, I will explain why people lie to themselves and how necessary stories are to deal with the deluge of information all consumers face every day.

People believe stories because they are compelling. We lie to ourselves about what we're about to buy. Consumers covet things that they believe will save them time or make them prettier or richer. And consumers know their own hot buttons better than any marketer can. So the consumer tells herself a story, an involved tale that explains how this new purchase will surely answer her deepest needs.

An hour ago, I watched a story transform the face of Stephanie, a physical therapist who should know better. Stephanie was about to buy a pair of limited edition sneakers from Puma: $125 for the pair, about what she earns, after tax, after a long day of hard work.

Was Stephanie thinking about support or sole material or the durability of the uppers? Of course not. She was imagining how she'd look when she put them on. She was visualizing her dramatically improved life once other people saw how cool she was. She was embracing the idea that she was a grown-up, a professional who could buy a ridiculously priced pair of sneakers if she wanted to. In other words, she was busy lying to herself, telling herself a story.

The way Stephanie *felt* when she bought the Pumas *was* the product. Not the sneakers (made for $3 in China). She could have bought adequate footwear for a fraction of what the Pumas cost. What the marketers sold her was a story, a story that made her feel special. Stories (not ideas, not features, not benefits) are what spread from person to person.

Make no mistake—this was not an accident. Puma works hard to tell a story. It's a story about hipness and belonging and fashion—and it has built its entire business around the ability to tell this story.

TELLING A GREAT STORY

Truly great stories succeed because they are able to capture the imagination of large or important audiences.

A great story is true. Not true because it's factual, but true because it's consistent and authentic. Consumers are too good at sniffing out inconsistencies for a marketer to get away with a story that's just slapped on. When the Longaberger Corporation built its headquarters to look like a giant basket, it was living its obsession with the product—a key part of its story.

Great stories make a promise. They promise fun or money, safety or a shortcut. The promise is bold and audacious and not just very good—it's exceptional or it's not worth listening to. Phish offered its legions of fans a completely different concert experience. The promise of a transcendental evening of live music allowed the group to reach millions of listeners who easily ignored the pablum pouring out of their radios. Phish made a promise, and even better, kept that promise.

Great stories are trusted. Trust is the scarcest resource we've got left. No one trusts anyone. Consumers don't trust the beautiful women ordering vodka at the corner bar (they're getting paid by the liquor company). Consumers don't trust the spokespeople on commercials (who exactly is Rula Lenska?) and consumers don't trust the companies that make pharmaceuticals (Vioxx, apparently, can kill you). As a result, no marketer succeeds in telling a story unless he has earned the credibility to tell that story.

Great stories are subtle. Surprisingly, the less a marketer spells out, the more powerful the story becomes. Talented marketers understand that the prospect is ultimately telling *himself* the lie, so allowing him (and the rest of the target audience) to draw his own conclusions is far more effective than just announcing the punch line.

Great stories happen fast. They engage the consumer the moment the story clicks into place. First impressions are far more powerful than we give them credit for. Great stories don't always need eight-page color brochures or a face-to-face meeting. Great stories match the voice the consumer's worldview was seeking, and they sync right up with her expectations. Either you are ready to listen to what a Prius delivers or you aren't.

Great stories don't appeal to logic, but they often appeal to our senses. Pheromones aren't a myth. People decide if they like someone after just a sniff. And the design of an Alessi teapot talks to consumers in a way that a fact sheet about boiling water never could.

Great stories are rarely aimed at everyone. Average people are good at ignoring you. Average people have too many different points of view about life and average people are by and large satisfied. If you need to water down your story to appeal to everyone, it will appeal to no one. Runaway hits like the LiveStrong fund-raising bracelets take off because they match the worldview of a tiny audience—and then that tiny audience spreads the story.

Great stories don't contradict themselves. If your restaurant is in the right location but has the wrong menu, you lose. If your art gallery carries the right artists but your staff is rejects from a used car lot, you lose. If your subdivision has lovely wooded grounds but ticky-tacky McMansions, you lose. Consumers are clever and they'll see through your deceit at once.

And most of all, great stories agree with our worldview. The best stories don't teach people anything new. Instead, the best stories agree with what the audience already believes and makes the members of the audience feel smart and secure when reminded how right they were in the first place.

TELLING A STORY BADLY: THE PLIGHT OF THE TELEMARKETER

It's 5:30. I've got three pots boiling on the stove and dinner is in twenty minutes. The phone rings.

A quick glance at the caller ID screen shows me a number and an area code that I'm not familiar with. The text ID says, "AAATeleServices." I'm already telling myself a story.

The lie I'm telling myself isn't pretty. It's a detailed monologue about someone trying to steal my time, to rip me off, to deal with me dishonestly. I remind myself that even answering the phone puts my number on a list of names worth selling to someone else. Still, I chance it.

"Hello?"

My story is confirmed in less than a second. First I hear the telltale click of a dial-ahead computer-aided system passing me off to the next operator in line. Then I hear the unique bustle and background noise of a boiler room operation. Before the operator even opens his mouth, the story is previewed, told and sold. I'm not interested.

For research purposes, I hang on instead of hanging up.

The operator starts giving a prewritten speech. He doesn't stop for at least ten sentences. He's reading a script and he's not doing a particularly good job of it. The words don't match his unsophisticated tone of voice.

I'm long gone, of course. But the final straw is when he starts saying things that are patently and transparently untrue. "I'm with the New York State Police Chief's Association and we're raising money for the benevolent fund."

Is it any wonder that more than 50,000,000 people signed on to the Do Not Call Registry in just a matter of weeks? If a telemarketer has a story to tell, most of us don't want to hear it.

TELLING A STORY WELL: KIEHL'S SINCE 1851

About twenty years ago, long before online shopping, a colleague in Boston asked me to stop by Kiehl's Since 1851, an obscure drugstore in Manhattan. She explained that it had a special skin lotion she loved, and always eager to please, I volunteered to head a few blocks out of my way one day to pick some up.

I walked into the store not knowing a thing about Kiehl's, but curious about why someone would insist on a skin cream only available two hundred miles away from home. The first thing I saw when I walked into the tiny store was a Ducati motorcycle and a tiny stunt airplane.

Now I was officially intrigued. Why was this expensive real estate devoted to housing items that clearly had nothing whatsoever to do with skin care? The rest of the store was just as interesting. The rough-hewn floors were at least a hundred years old. The staff was far better trained than I'd ever expected to find in a drugstore. The labels were filled with information and each item was lovingly displayed.

The message was loud and clear: this is the work of a person, a unique individual, not a corporation.

Only a person would waste so much space on his hobbies (and it had to be a him, it seemed to me). Only a person would be so persnickety about the formulas and the labels and the making everything just right. In a marketplace filled with anonymous competitors, this was the real deal—genuine cosmetics made by someone who cared.

The store was filled with other tidbits of information. Detailed narratives about animal testing and motorcycle racing, about the founders and about their customers. The prices were ridiculous, the bottles unlike any I'd ever seen sold for money (they appeared homemade—and still do). I bought my colleague her cream and headed for home, but not before I'd bought myself some shave cream and my wife a bar of soap. And just like a little family business, they insisted on giving me samples of other products to take home—for free.

Apparently many others have had a similar experience. Kiehl's Since 1851 is now a cult brand. Sold by exclusive, service-oriented shops around the world, this business is doing many millions of dollars a year in high-margin sales. The story is compelling. It's easy to believe the lie we tell ourselves. So easy to believe that most of its customers are shocked when they discover that industry giant L'Oréal has owned the company for several years.

Is the brand worth the premium they charge consumers? Well, if worth is measured in the price charged compared to the cost of the raw ingredients, of course not. But if Kiehl's customers are measuring the price paid compared to the experience of purchasing and the way that using the product makes them feel, it's a no-brainer.

Is Kiehl's for everyone? Not yet. Only people with a certain worldview even notice Kiehl's, and then it takes a subset of that group to fall in love with the story, to tell itself the lie. These people embrace the brand and tell the story to their friends as well. If a consumer believes that cosmetics should be cheap or ubiquitous or the brand that a best friend uses, then Kiehl's is invisible. But if a consumer's worldview is about finding something offbeat, unique and aggressively original, then the story resonates.

Ironically Kiehl's didn't set out to succeed by telling a unique story. This brand is the work of an idiosyncratic individual, and lucky for him, his story meshed with the worldview of the people who shopped there. **In other words, it wasn't Kiehl doing the marketing—it was his customers. Kiehl's told a story, and the customers told the lie to themselves and to their friends.**

THE ACCIDENTAL MARKETER

Who made granola healthy?

Certainly not the Granola Manufacturers of America, a fictional organization I just dreamed up. Nor was it Quaker or Alpen. The facts of the case are simple: most granola is loaded with sugar and saturated fats. It's not good for you at all. But consumers decided it was a healthy, hippy, new-wave, nutritious, back-to-nature snack, the sort of thing you took with you on hikes in the woods or ate for breakfast at a spa.

Sure, the big marketers came in after consumers believed the story, and they were quick to take advantage of it. They launched all sorts of boxes and brands and ads—the expensive kind of marketing. But long before business school tactics took over, the granola story established one thing with certainty: **consumers are complicit in marketing.** Consumers believe stories. Without this belief, there is no marketing. A marketer can spend plenty on promoting a product, but unless consumers are actively engaged in believing the story, nothing happens.

MARKETERS AREN'T REALLY LIARS

I wasn't being completely truthful with you when I named this book. Marketers aren't liars. They are just storytellers. It's the consumers who are liars. As consumers, we lie to ourselves every day. We lie to ourselves about what we wear, where we live, how we vote and what we do at work. **Successful marketers are just the providers of stories that consumers choose to believe.**

This is a book about the psychology of satisfaction. I believe that people tell themselves stories and then work hard to make them true. I call a story that a consumer believes a *lie*. I think that once people find a remarkable lie that will benefit them if it spreads, they selfishly tell the lie to others, embellishing it along the way.

A good story (either from the marketer or from the customer herself) is where genuine customer satisfaction comes from. It's the source of growth and profit and it's the future of your organization. Maybe who is lying to whom isn't all that important, in the end, as long as the connection has been made and the story has been successfully told.

THIS APPEARS TO BE A BOOK ABOUT LYING

But the irony, of course, is that it's a book about telling (and living) the truth.

The only way your story will be believed, the only way people will tell themselves the lie you are depending on and the only way your idea will spread is **if you tell the**

truth. And you are telling the truth when you live the story you are telling—when it's *authentic.*

The best stories marketers tell turn out to be true. Go to a product development meeting at Nike or sit in on a recording session at Blue Note or spend some time with Pat Robertson—none of these marketers are sitting around scheming up new plans on how to deceive the public. Instead, they are living and breathing their stories. Not only are they lying to the public, they're lying to themselves.

This is what makes it all work: *a complete dedication to and embrace of your story*.

ONE LAST THING BEFORE WE GET GOING: KNOW YOUR POWER

I believe marketing is the most powerful force available to people who want to make change. And with that power comes responsibility. We (anyone with the ability to tell a story—online, in print or to the people in our communities) have the ability to change things more dramatically than ever before in history. Marketers have the leverage to generate huge impact in less time—and with less money—than ever before.

There's no question that consumers (and voters and nations, and so on) are complicit in this storytelling process. No marketer can get a person to do something without his active participation. But this complicity doesn't absolve marketers of the responsibility that comes with the awesome power we've got to tell and spread stories.

The question you have to ask yourself is this: what are you going to do with that power?

GOT MARKETING?

DOES MARKETING MATTER?

When you think of marketing, do you think of Wisk, Super Bowl commercials or perhaps an annoying yet catchy slogan? Do images of used-car salesmen pop into your head? Or worse, do you think of relentless spam and clueless telemarketers?

Marketing has become far more than an old lady crying, "Where's the beef!" Stuff like that is just a tactic.

Marketing is about spreading ideas, and spreading ideas is the single most important output of our civilization. Hundreds of thousands of Sudanese have died because of bad marketing. Religions thrive or fade away because of the marketing choices they make. Children are educated, companies are built, jobs are gained or lost—all because of what we know (and don't know) about spreading ideas.

Am I trivializing these important events by implying that marketing is at the heart of the issue? I don't think so. I think that commercials and hype trivialized marketing, but in fact, my definition of marketing casts a much wider net. These issues are too important *not* to be marketed.

It's easy for the media and the public to focus on a small child trapped in a well or on a wacky auction on eBay. Some ideas spread far and wide and have a huge impact—while others, ideas even more valuable and urgent, seem to fade away. If marketers could tell a better story about the really urgent stuff—taking your medicine or sending peacekeepers where they belong—we would all benefit.

If you care about the future of your company, your nonprofit, your church or your planet, marketing matters. Marketing matters because whether or not you're in a position to buy a commercial, if you've got an idea to spread, you're now a marketer.

Key fact: in 2003 pharmaceutical companies spent more on marketing and sales than they did on research and development. When it comes time to invest, it's pretty clear that spreading the ideas behind the medicine is more important than inventing the medicine itself.

BEFORE, DURING AND AFTER THE GOLDEN AGE

Before the golden age of television, marketing wasn't particularly important. Companies made commodities—things that people needed. If you could make something that answered a need, was fairly priced and well distributed, you'd do just fine.

Farmers didn't worry too much about marketing corn. Blacksmiths knew they'd do well if they could shoe a horse for a fair price. And the local barber cut hair. People bought stuff they needed and those with a skill made money providing for their customers' needs.

During the golden age, if you had enough money, you could buy a ton of television commercials and magazine ads and tell the story of your choice to each and every consumer. But you had to market to all the consumers at once—there were only three channels, after all.

You had sixty seconds to tell a simple story, and if you did a good job, you could create demand. Instead of satisfying a need, you could actually create a *want*.

"Plop, plop, fizz, fizz, oh what a relief it is."
"Ring around the collar!"
"You're soaking in it."

Television was a miracle. It enabled companies with money to effortlessly create more money. Consumers would gladly pay extra for Tony the Tiger or would wait in line to see the new 1954 Chevrolet.

To grow your company, all you had to do was create a commercial that generated demand—and then make something to sell. Businesses quickly recalibrated and fell in love with what they thought was marketing—using commercials to sell more stuff.

Marketers had a great run. Truly average products were sold for significant markups because of good advertising. Entire industries were born, stores were invented (the supermarket) just to sell the things that were now in demand because of commercials.

This was the age of the mass market, when all consumers were equal and you could sell anything to everyone. The best brands told stories, but all products with decent ads made money.

Then it all fell apart.

In a heartbeat, television commercials ceased to be the one-stop shop for all marketers. As consumers, we realized that we don't trust commercials, we don't watch them and we've got so many other ways to hear stories that they've lost their effectiveness. At the same time, though, marketing now is more powerful than it has ever been. That's because the new techniques have even more impact—because they're more subtle.

If you aren't doing as well as you'd like, it's probably because you're acting like the golden age is still here. It's not. In the last century, marketers fell in love with telling stories via commercials on television, and we forgot about other, more effective ways to spread our ideas.

After the golden age, in what should be marketing's darkest hour, the industry has reinvented itself. This is a book about the new kind of marketing. It's about telling stories, not buying commercials.

Marketing is the story marketers tell to consumers, and then maybe, if the marketer has done a good job, the lie consumers tell themselves and their friends. Those stories are no longer reserved for television commercials or junk mail. They are everywhere.

Some marketers focus so hard on the facts of their offering that they forget to tell a story at all, and then wonder why they've failed. I've spent the last year thinking about why some things spread and others don't. Why do some organizations start strong and then falter, while others can gradually grow in importance and profit and keep it going forever?

Marketers can no longer use commercials to tell their stories. Instead they have to live them.

Yes, marketing matters. It matters so much that we have an obligation to do it right. Marketing has become more powerful than it has ever been before. It's not an overstatement to say that marketing changes the world on a daily basis. I think it's time we figured out how to make it work the way it should.

WHEN YOU KNOW THE SECRET, THINGS LOOK DIFFERENT

In the East Village, there's a wildly popular bar and nightclub called Lucky Cheng's. It's filled with boisterous people, whooping and hollering and having quite a good time. At first you don't notice exactly what's different about this place. Sure, the waitresses appear to be trying a bit harder, wearing nicer outfits and vamping it up a bit. But still . . .

Until you notice that the waitresses are actually men.

Then everything changes. Not the bar, not the drinks, not the patrons. What changes is the way you look at the place, because you know the trick—you know how they did it.

Well there's a secret about marketing that this book is going to reveal to you. Once you know the secret, every successful company will look different. You'll understand (perhaps for the first time) that there is a complete disconnect between observable reality and the lies we tell ourselves. There is almost no connection between what is actually *there* and what we *believe*—whether you're talking about hospital cribs, soup, computers, people, cars or just about any product or service we buy at work or at home.

(Note: when I write *company*, feel free to insert *church*, *nonprofit, campaign, PTA, job seeker* or whatever other entity is relevant to you. We all tell stories, every day, and this book is about your story too.)

HOW MARKETING WORKS (WHEN IT WORKS)

Most marketing fails. I want to show you what marketing is like when it works. Here are the steps that people go through when they encounter successful marketing. The rest of this book is organized into sections built around each of these ideas:

STEP 1: THEIR WORLDVIEW AND FRAMES GOT THERE BEFORE YOU DID

A consumer's worldview affects the way he notices things and understands them. If a story is framed in terms of that worldview, he's more likely to believe it.

STEP 2: PEOPLE ONLY NOTICE THE NEW AND THEN MAKE A GUESS

Consumers notice something only when it changes.

STEP 3: FIRST IMPRESSIONS START THE STORY

A first impression causes the consumer to make a very quick, permanent judgment about what he was just exposed to.

STEP 4: GREAT MARKETERS TELL STORIES WE BELIEVE

The marketer tells a story about what the consumer notices. The story changes the way the consumer experiences the product or service and he tells himself a lie.

Consumers make a prediction about what will happen next.

Consumers rationalize anything that doesn't match that prediction.

STEP 5: MARKETERS WITH AUTHENTICITY THRIVE

The authenticity of the story determines whether it will survive scrutiny long enough for the consumer to tell the story to other people.

Sometimes marketing is so powerful it can actually change the worldview of someone who experiences it, but no marketing succeeds if it can't find an audience that already wants to believe the story being told.

YOU'RE NOT IN CHARGE (PEOPLE *CAN'T* LISTEN)

The biggest myth marketers believe: "I have money, which means that I am in charge. I have control over the conversation, over the airwaves, over your attention and over retailers."

You, the marketer, are *not* in charge.

You are not in charge of attention or the conversations or even the stories you tell. Until marketers of all stripes realize this, marketing will never come near its potential to change things.

There's too much to say and not enough time to say it in. New and Improved and Organic and Healthy and Union-made and Calorie-free and Low-carb and Celebrity-endorsed and As-Seen-On-TV and so on. You've heard the numbing statistics about new product introductions and media clutter so often that you've forgotten just how bad they are.

Not only are there too many choices, but as products and services have gotten more and more complex, there's a lot of teaching for marketers to do. Alas, there's no time to do it. Marketers need to teach consumers why their new product is worth the premium they need to charge, why their new formula is a breakthrough and why consumers should abandon what they're using today.

There are more and more competitors blocking you from getting your voice heard, allowing you to increase your share of consumer attention. And there are more and more media alternatives keeping you from telling your story to the masses.

As a result, people pick and choose. *Everyone will not listen to everything.*

Some people will hear part of your message and make an assumption about what your product does. Other people will ignore that part and instead focus on the way your logo makes them feel. And a third group will ignore all that and just look at the price.

Even if we could be sure of the magic phrase that would turn a prospect into a customer, we can't use it because we don't know which customer is going to listen to which message. It's not crisp. It's fuzzy.

YOU'RE NOT IN CHARGE (YOU CAN'T CONTROL THE CONVERSATION)

Most messages don't come from marketers.

Yes, it's a myth that you're in charge. That John Kerry gets to decide what people will hear and learn about him, that Dell or Allstate or Mini or Maytag are somehow in control of everything that gets received by the ultimate consumer of the product.

In the business-to-business marketing world (and medicine too) this conceit is even worse. We'd like to believe that people are rational and informed. They are neither.

Positioning by Jack Trout and Al Ries is one of the most important marketing books ever. And it's a great start. But it's only a start. Positioning, as practiced by most people, is one dimensional. If they are cheap, we're expensive. They are fast, we are slow, and so on.

The authors want you to choose a position for your product knowing that the consumer will receive the position you choose to send them. That's the way it worked in the old days, when a commercial could deliver precisely the story you hoped it would.

Yes, you must choose a position. (Or it will be chosen for you.) But no, you don't get to control the message. And no, a one-dimensional message isn't enough. Most learning about products and services and politicians goes on outside of existing paid marketing channels. You don't have to like that fact, but as the saying goes, you can look it up.

Positioning in the world of the story is a longer, subtler, more involved process. It's three dimensional and it goes on forever.

YOU'RE NOT IN CHARGE (IT WON'T STAY STABLE!)

Every message changes the marketplace.

Just as in evolutionary biology, the game is always changing. The evolutionary paradox called the curse of the Red Queen states that what worked yesterday is unlikely to work today. When Alice was busy playing chess in Wonderland, the Red Queen kept changing the game whenever she moved. The same thing occurs in our marketing wonderland. One competitor makes a change and suddenly the entire competitive landscape is different.

The reason marketing seems irrational and inconsistent and faddy is that it is. It is because unlike most business functions, the actions of our competitors (and our actions as well) change what's going to work in the future. That doesn't make it safe, but it seems to keep it interesting.

MAKE STUFF UP: THE NEW POWER CURVE

If you ask most of your coworkers what they are particularly skilled and productive at while at work, the answers will be pretty similar. They will talk about tasks that create a physical output. Bending metal. Filling out forms. Creating spreadsheets. Managers will tell you how well they manage the day-to-day crises that cross their desks. Résumés confirm this—the organization of our organizations is all about getting stuff done and smart job seekers stress this in their credentials.

That's no surprise. The old power curve is on the next page.

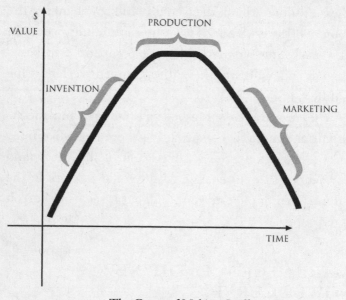

The Curve of Making Stuff

All the juicy stuff was in the middle. The center of the curve had the most value, because that's where the profit was. If you ran an efficient factory and made quality products and shipped on time, your advertising would take care of the rest. Make good stuff for cheap, that was the motto.

The unsung heroes were the factory foremen and the quality control guys. Sure, it helped if you had a terrific invention, but those were easy to copy. And it was terrific if you had a powerful brand, but those lasted forever and over time, people could inch up on you.

That's why résumés read the way they do. Why we

learn what we learn in school: the old power curve rewarded people who *did* stuff.

The new power curve looks like this:

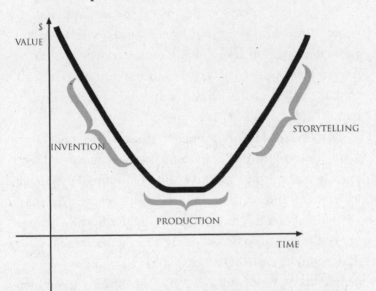

The Curve of Making Stuff Up

Product and service life cycles are much shorter now, so the quality of the original idea (and the story it can tell) matter a great deal. Very few organizations can now grow and thrive by creating a new kind of commodity and producing it cheaply. A remarkable product is much easier to make a profit on if you can get it to market before the competition.

I call this the Talerman curve after my friend Elizabeth. She's making a profit with a line of clever T-shirts and

with fashionable serving bowls. In both cases, it's the original idea and the storytelling—not the craftsmanship of the
outsourced item itself—that's building her business.

Because it's so easy to outsource the actual manufacturing, suddenly your plant foreman isn't your most important asset. Southwest doesn't succeed or fail because
of its pilots—pilots are easy to find and hire now. It's easy
to make ball bearings, T-shirts, bottled water and mort-
gages. *Making* isn't hard any more.

Ford makes Jaguars, Anheuser-Busch makes Kirin, an
anonymous plant in Vietnam makes Nike sneakers. The
making isn't hard or special or differentiating any longer.

And the end of the curve, the place where you actually tell your stories and authentically live up to what you
say you're going to do—that's where the leverage is now.
The right side of the curve, where you take something
people may or may not need and turn it into something
they definitely want—that's where the money is.

There are only two things that separate success from
failure in most organizations today:

1. Invent stuff worth talking about.
2. Tell stories about what you've invented.

Make up great stories. That's the new motto.

This is *urgent*. The transformation of our organizations has been under way for a while, but now, thanks to

outsourcing and computers and increasing manufacturing quality, it's easier than it's ever been to get something made, shipped and stocked. Easier than ever to ensure quality and durability. What's difficult—really difficult—is figuring out what's worth making and then telling a story about it.

(*No*, I'm not saying that manufacturing doesn't matter. It does. It's an essential part of the story you're going to tell. I'm just saying it's not difficult, and that being good enough at manufacturing isn't good enough anymore.)

The reason most of the people who sell services and products to business are struggling with profit margins is that they see themselves as peddling a commodity. Because they focus on the center of the curve, on making a better widget a little cheaper, they're stuck. The organizations that succeed realize that offering a remarkable product with a great story is more important and more profitable than doing what everyone else is doing just a bit better.

On a personal level, your résumé should be about inventing remarkable things and telling stories that register—not about how good you are at meeting specs. Organizations that are going to be around tomorrow will be those that stop spending all their time dealing with the day-to-day crises of shipping stuff out the door or re-acting to emergencies. Instead the new way of marketing will separate winners from losers.

That's your challenge. The winners will be those who figure it out.

STEP 1:
THEIR WORLDVIEW
AND FRAMES GOT
THERE BEFORE
YOU DID

WE ALL WANT THE SAME THINGS

We all want to be safe, healthy, successful, loved, re-spected, happy and fit. We all want to have enough money to buy whatever we want. We all want friends and fun and a clean world to enjoy them in.

But if we all want the same thing, why do we take so many opposite tacks to get there? Why doesn't every-one drive a Honda or run their factory using the same techniques? Why don't we all practice the same religion and wear the same clothes? Why is the average price paid for a wedding dress $799—with some women pay-ing ten or twenty times that and others borrowing one for free?

The great failure of marketing theory is its inability to explain variety. No marketer can tell you in advance if an advertisement is going to work or if a new product is going to be successful. As a result, the whole thing feels like a crapshoot.

The explanation for this variety lies in the worldview all consumers carry around. It turns out that **we don't all want the same things!** Each person has a different set of biases and values and assumptions, and those worldviews are influenced by their parents, their schools, the places they live and the experiences they've had to date. Their worldview is the lens they use to determine whether or not they're going to believe a story. As the great Red Maxwell said, "Lenses distort things." The lens your consumers use shows them a different version of reality than it shows you or your colleagues or your other customers.

TWO DEFINITIONS AND A STRATEGY

Worldview is the term I use to refer to the rules, values, beliefs and biases that an individual consumer brings to a situation.

If Jason got completely screwed the last time he bought a car from a used-car salesman, the worldview he has when visiting a dealership four years later is a little different than that of someone who is buying her third car in four years from the same place.

If Rebecca sees her job as purchasing agent for a big

company as one where she should avoid risks, she'll view that new salesperson in her office very differently than if her understanding of her job is that she should cut costs by innovating and trying new alternatives.

Different people, different worldviews. People can see the same data and make a totally different decision.

Frames are elements of a story painted to leverage the worldview a consumer already has. George Lakoff popularized this term in his writing about political discourse, but it applies to anything that's marketed to anyone.

Krispy Kreme did it with the phrase *Hot Donuts*. *Hot* means fresh and sensual and decadent. Pile that onto the way some of us feel about donuts and they had tapped into an existing worldview (donuts = sensual = hot = love). It wouldn't work on everyone, but until people changed their worldview (donuts = carbs = get fat), they did great. Today Krispy Kreme is losing money, shutting stores and facing government inquiries—all because of a change in worldview.

A frame, in other words, is a way you hang a story on to a consumer's existing worldview.

When a furniture store runs a going out of business sale with banners on every street corner, they're not talking about the furniture. They are framing the story for people who need an excuse to get their cheap spouse to finally get up and go with them to shop for furniture. This frame works on some people, but not on the folks who drive two hundred miles to an antique fair or redecorate whenever Martha tells them to. Different worldviews, different frames.

Don't try to change someone's worldview is the strategy smart marketers follow. Don't try to use facts to prove your case and to insist that people change their biases. You don't have enough time and you don't have enough money. Instead, identify a population with a certain worldview, frame your story in terms of that worldview and you win.

ALL SQUIRRELS WANT NUTS

If you want to attract some squirrels, put out some acorns. It's a safe bet.

Nuts are something that squirrels need, the same way people need water and food. But once we start talking about more sophisticated products, things that people *want* instead of need, the discussion gets complicated. Even extremely poor consumers in the developing world will prioritize their purchases to get what they want, often ignoring the opportunity to take what they need.

It's easy to fall into the trap of thinking of your market as a cohesive audience, of thinking of a market as a large group of similar people. But there is no monolith of want.

Everyone doesn't want a slightly better dishwasher or

a faster plane ride. Not enough to pay extra for it, any-way. We don't all want dark chocolate or a big house in the suburbs.

As the number of choices facing consumers increases, and the diversity of education, backgrounds and desires increases as well, it's awfully dangerous to assume that consumers are all the same—it's even dangerous to as-sume that they're all rational.

THEY SAY THERE'S NO ACCOUNTING FOR TASTE . . .

But of course there is. Taste is another word for a per-son's worldview.

In the 2004 presidential election, 290 million people all had access to the same data. We all had the same look at the same two candidates. Yet about half of us were sure that one guy was better and the other half disagreed. Can 145 million people be wrong? I don't think so. Instead I believe that there are dozens or even hundreds of world-views among voters. These views were entrenched long before the campaigning even started.

A vote is a statement about the voter, not the candidate.

Worldviews are the reason that two intelligent people can look at the same data and walk away with completely different conclusions—it's not that they didn't have access to the data or that they have poor reasoning skills, it's simply that they had already put themselves into a particular worldview before you even asked the question.

Marketing succeeds when enough people with similar worldviews come together in a way that allows marketers to reach them cost-effectively.

But what about *changing* a worldview? What about creating wholesale changes in the marketplace? Sometimes a marketer is particularly fortunate and skillful and she actually causes a big chunk of the marketplace to change its worldview. Steve Jobs did this with the Macintosh and then with the iPod. Shawn Fanning, founder of Napster, taught an entire generation of kids to believe that music is supposed to be free. It's interesting to note that while changing a worldview is fairly glamorous work, it doesn't often lead to a lot of profit.

Marketers don't hesitate to run different ads for men and women, for the rich and the poor, for those that travel and those that don't. The mistake is that we don't go far enough. There isn't one market. There are a million markets, each filled with people who share a worldview. The most successful, fastest-moving examples are those where the marketer used a frame to leverage an existing worldview, not to change one. **Your opportunity lies in finding a neglected worldview, framing your story in a way that this audience will focus on and going from there.**

WHAT COLOR ARE YOUR GLASSES?

We are not all the same.

The mass market is dead. Instead we are faced with collections of individuals. We may all be created equal, but our worldviews are different. Long before a person is exposed to a particular marketing message, she's already begun to tell herself a story.

A Republican's first look at a Democratic presidential candidate is very different than a Democrat's. Silicon Valley venture capitalists looked at eBay with expectations that were completely different than those of a similar firm in Hartford.

As the number of choices in every marketplace increases, the power of the consumer to indulge her worldview increases just as quickly. To go to market without understanding your audience's various worldviews is like trying to pick a lock without bothering to notice whether it uses a key or a combination.

> A worldview is not who you are. It's what you believe. It's your biases.
>
> A worldview is not forever. It's what the consumer believes *right now*.

Marketing succeeds when it taps into an audience of people who share a worldview—a worldview that makes that audience inclined to believe the story the marketer tells. Marketing success stories (Starbucks, *Fast Company*, the Porsche Cayenne) occur when that shared worldview is discovered for the first time.

WHO WE ARE AFFECTS WHAT WE SEE

The story a consumer tells himself about a new product or service is primarily influenced by the worldview that consumer had before he even knew about the new thing. That worldview affects three things:

1. *Attention:* the consumer's worldview determines whether she even bothers to pay attention. If she doesn't think she needs a new brand of aspirin or a faster computer, she's far less likely to notice a new one when it appears.
2. *Bias:* everyone carries around a list of grudges and wishes. When a new product or service appears on your horizon, those predispositions instantly color all the information that comes in.
3. *Vernacular:* consumers care just as much about *how* something is said as *what* is said. They care about the choice of media, the tone of voice, the words that are used—even the way things smell. When the story that's told to the consumer doesn't match the vernacular the consumer expects, weird things happen.

Understanding how worldviews interfere with or amplify the story a marketer tells is the most overlooked element of marketing success. Until now it's been intuitive. Marketers need to figure out how to get it right every time.

GLIMPSES OF A WORLDVIEW

Do you agree with these statements?

- New technology can improve my life.
- If I was prettier, I'd be more popular.
- If it's a prescription medicine, it's probably safe.
- I can afford the best.
- All car salesmen are liars.
- I need some new clothes.
- I like opera.
- It's possible that a product advertised on an infomercial might be a good buy.
- My goal is to tread lightly on the Earth.
- I love the New York Yankees.
- Physical therapy will cure me faster than surgery will.
- Protecting my family from harm is the most important thing I can do.
- Let's party!
- Don't tell me shallow stories about consumerism and flash and spend, spend, spend. Talk to me about inner values, quality and life.

Regardless of "reality" (as determined by double-blind studies, extensive research or a cold, hard look at the facts), the statements above are easily believed or disbelieved by different individuals. Add them (and a thousand others) all up and you've defined the biases that a particular consumer brings to the table.

This seems obvious, doesn't it? It does to me. It seems really clear that everyone is different and those differences explain what we pay attention to and what we ignore. Yet just about every marketer (job seeker, non-profit, political candidate, beer manufacturer, and so on) treats every consumer as a potential customer. Not just a potential customer, but a potential customer who is just like all the other potential customers out there.

Of course, all customers are not the same, but they're not all different either. **People clump together into common worldviews, and your job is to find a previously undiscovered clump and frame a story for those people.**

1,000 WORLDVIEWS

There are new mothers who believe that happiness lies in the next new educational product for their infant, and there are bodybuilders who believe that the next nutritional supplement will provide them the shortcut to a perfect body. There are environmentalists who are certain that the next scientific innovation will be mankind's last, and xenophobes who know for sure that black helicopters from the United Nations are due to arrive tomorrow.

Each of these groups wants to hear stories that support its worldview. Each group (and they're not mutually exclusive—some of those new moms are also conspiracy theorists) sees itself as near the center, not on the fringe, and each group very much wants to be catered to.

Baby Einstein, a division of Disney, sold more than $150 million worth of videos for newborns and infants last year, providing a virtually useless product to women who wanted to hear a story that matched their worldview. They bought the story, believed the lie and shared the story with anyone else who would listen to their word of mouth about teaching infants with videotapes. The people who buy the Baby Einstein videos are complicit in the storytelling that the company does.

Soon the product leaves the obsessed group and becomes part of our culture. You don't have to be part of the original fan group to want to buy the video for your baby now. You do it because your neighbors expect you to. (And that means the video isn't useless—sure, it's useless for babies, but it satisfies a real desire for the parents.)

Aren't these just niche markets? After all, hot sauce addicts and NASCAR fans and chowhounds are nothing but established, if small, markets. It turns out that worldview thinking offers you a much bigger opportunity: the ability to find overlooked big markets by clumping together people with complementary worldviews.

Often a shared worldview is not an entire market, just part of one—and treating each subset of a market with respect to its worldview is essential if you want to be successful in framing and telling a story.

When premium tea came to the United States, there appeared to be no market for it. People in focus groups weren't asking for it, there wasn't a big demand for it in gourmet stores and most market researchers would tell you that Americans weren't ready to spend more than the cost of Tetley for a cup of tea.

If you insisted on treating all potential tea drinkers the same (as Tetley and Lipton did) then you'd lose. Celestial Seasonings had demonstrated that hippies would buy herbal tea, but that was truly a niche.

It took brands like the Republic of Tea and Tazo to prove the experts wrong. What these brands discovered, quite profitably, was that there was a significant number of people who share a worldview that said, "I don't want to drink coffee right now, but it would make me feel good to spend something extra to get a hot drink that's really special—that would make me feel like a connoisseur. A treat, because I'm not like the rest of the crowd and I'm worth it."

That's exactly the worldview these brands were framed

around. They told a complicated story about origins and health and flavor and brewing, and the previously ignored community woke up and paid attention. They framed the tea story like the detailed stories so many people believe about wine and convinced a substantial portion of the tea *and* coffee markets to believe the story.

Not all ignored worldviews are markets in waiting. They're either too small or too fearful or too much at the fringe. But there are countless groups that are so far being ignored, mainly because conventional wisdom has always ignored them.

Some of these groups may be small, but they can take your story and run with it. They can turn a small market into a cult, into a movement and then a trend, and finally into a mass market.

THE POWER OF FRAMES

While targeting the right worldview is essential, the real magic of marketing occurs when you use a frame. A frame allows you to present an idea in a way that embraces the consumer's worldview, not fights it.

Frames aren't just a tactic. Frames go to the heart of what marketing is today. If you're unable to tack your idea onto a person's worldview, then that idea will be ignored. *File sharing* is different from *stealing*. A picture of Houston's polluted waters and dead birds is just as accurate as one of Houston's skyscrapers and busy shopping malls, but they tell very different stories to very different people. *Firearm safety* is different from *banning handguns*, but both phrases are used to advance political agendas.

Frames are the words and images and interactions that reinforce a bias someone is already feeling. The media uses frames all the time when telling us stories. When the newspaper calls someone a "UFO buff" or a "conspiracy theorist," they're making it easy for the rest of us to believe that this group is marginal. Politicians are becoming masters of using frames to tell their stories. You pick: "fanatical right-wing fundamentalists" or "people of deeply held beliefs." Each phrase is easy to embrace for a community that shares a worldview.

GETTING IN THE DOOR

Speaking respectfully to a person's worldview is the price of entry to get their attention. If your message is framed in a way that conflicts with their worldview, you're invisible.

A frame is your first step in telling a persuasive story. I'm *not* recommending that you only tell people what they want to hear, that you pander to their worldview, that marketing is nothing but repeating what people already know. Far from it. Instead I believe the best marketing stories are told (and sold) with frames but ultimately spread to people who are open to being convinced of something brand new.

"NONE OF THE ABOVE"

Jimmy Carter was the exception that proved the rule.

Carter ran for president in much the same way Howard Dean did. He began by appealing to people who were disgusted with the system, who rejected the status quo, who had a worldview that embraced the choice of "none of the above."

This group obviously responds differently to a candidate than a lifelong Republican or Democrat would. The voters who choose "none of the above" see different things and tell themselves a different lie.

In European countries, this segment of the population is usually able to elect a few members to parliament. It rarely has much influence over policy, but it keeps things interesting. In the United States, though, this group of disaffected but slightly involved voters almost never gets the chance to elect the candidate of their choice as president.

Howard Dean saw this group as an opportunity. He told them a story ("I'm against the war in Iraq") and he differentiated himself immediately from most of his opponents. The lie that his target audience told themselves (thoughtful outsider who's just like us) was simple and conveniently ignored a wide range of facts, from geographic issues (Dean was from rural Vermont, not some bustling blue state city) to economic ones (Dean was actually quite financially conservative).

The word spread. It was an easy story to share. The none-of-the-above population was electrified and unified by his candidacy. They swamped meetup.com and filled the Internet with adoring blogs. They raised money and mailed letters.

The bet that Dean and his people were making was risky but straightforward. They were focused on engaging this group but they knew they had to make the leap from the none-of-the-above group to the general population. It's the leap you must make as well, when you go from introducing an item that's fashionable for one small but passionate group to a much larger group that doesn't share the same interests and prejudices of the first group.

This is precisely the same chasm that Geoffrey Moore talks about in *Crossing the Chasm:* moving from the early adopters to the mass market. What Moore misses is that this isn't a flat, simple curve. In fact, it's a multidimensional mess that occurs across populations and worldviews and markets.

Whether you're selling shoes or computers or a candidate, moving your story from one segment of the population to another is the hard part. Dean failed. He failed big and fast. The reason he failed was the very reason he succeeded at first: because he appealed to people who wanted to make a point, not to elect a candidate. The story that wiped out Dean? It was one word: unelectable. The none-of-the-above people were unable to persuade their Democratic friends that Dean could win the general election. The story stopped spreading and stalled.

Carter succeeded, but don't bet the lunch money that it will happen again. Insurgents in every market face the same challenge when trying to reach the mass market. You're more likely to succeed as long as you avoid winner-take-all contests.

It's so tempting to tell your story to an audience that desperately wants to hear it. The problem is that this audience may embrace your story but might not make you any money (or get you elected). **It's not enough to find a niche that shares a worldview. That niche has to be ready and able to influence a large group of their friends.**

ANGELS AND DEVILS

Best Buy is one of my favorite companies, because they combine an obsession with data with friendly people and real style. Their current move against the devils in their business can help you understand why you need to be choosy in selecting where you tell your story.

Like most mass merchants, Best Buy wants as many people walking through the store as possible. They rent in desirable retail locations, run millions of dollars' worth of ads and promotions and stock a wide range of products and price points.

Recently, though, Brad Anderson, Best Buy's CEO, discovered that 100 million (about 20 percent) of Best Buy's customers were actually costing the company money. If they could focus their energy on the other 80 percent, he figured the stores would be more fun to shop in and they would actually increase their profitability.

The problem is that Best Buy tells a story to two different audiences with two radically different worldviews.

The first audience (the angels) believes that shopping for consumer electronics is fun. They believe that owning the latest LCD projector or widescreen television is a luxury worth paying for. This audience relies on Best Buy for great service and a fun place to shop. They're not so price sensitive that they'll run over to Wal-Mart the first time they can save $30.

The second audience (the devils) believes that paying the absolutely lowest price is the entire point. Some members of this group will stoop as low as buying something, opening it and then returning it the next day to take advantage of Best Buy's generous return privileges. The returned item goes on the half-priced table, at which point the original purchaser comes back to the store and buys the item he had returned just a day earlier—saving himself 50 percent.

As you can imagine, these two audiences tell themselves very different stories about Best Buy. The angels see the circular in the newspaper and dream about what to buy themselves as a treat. The devils visit Web sites like SlickDeals.net and Techbargains.com, sites that are devoted to trading insider tips on how to take advantage of the store.

If you viewed all potential consumers the same, you'd be as happy to advertise on Techbargains.com as you might be in the *Dallas Morning News*. Yet just because someone wants to tell themselves a lie about what you stand for doesn't mean you should encourage it.

It may be counterintuitive, but Best Buy's decision to fire some customers and cater to those that share a profitable (and positive) worldview is exactly the right thing to do.

LUCKY CHARMS IS A HEALTH FOOD?

The cereal business had a great run. For more than twenty years, prices were raised, shelf space increased, profits went up and demand was steady.

Then Atkins hit. The worldview of a big chunk of the audience changed, almost overnight. Suddenly moms weren't so eager to relive their childhood by serving refined sugars and flours to their kids for breakfast. Interstate Bakeries, the folks that bring you Twinkies and Wonder Bread, went bankrupt. All of a sudden, the lies consumers told themselves about breakfast cereal and wholesomeness were under pressure.

Jay Gouliard (the guy who brought us Gogurt) and his team at General Mills saw the change and decided to take action. Less than one hundred days after they decided to change their story, every major cereal brand at General Mills was converted to 100 percent whole grain. Lucky Charms' new whole-grain formulation is a rapid response to a brand-new worldview: the awareness among an audience of parents that whole-grain food is a lot better for them and their kids. General Mills didn't invent Atkins, but once Atkins changed the bias of a large audience, General Mills was quick enough to tell a story to those people—while they were still listening.

Four things make General Mills' response likely to work: First, they did it quickly, so they stood out by being first. Second, the cereal still tastes great. And third, they leveraged the stories that have worked for so long ("magically delicious!") to give the new story weight. Finally, and most important, the new frame they are hanging around their old brands will find a large audience that shares the low-carb worldview.

Jay and his team understood how to use frames to tell a different story about a treasured brand. They told a story, we believed a lie and the word is spreading.

ATTENTION, BIAS AND VERNACULAR

ATTENTION

This is the unstated precious commodity. Consumers don't notice anything until they pay attention and *pay* is the perfect word. Everyone is granted a finite amount of time per day, and how it gets used is a significant decision. Some choose to pay that attention to the stock market, making themselves aware of every tremor and ripple in the Dow. Others use that time to study *Vogue*, becoming experts in heels and hems. Still others choose to ignore just about anything unsolicited, focusing instead on the interpersonal activities in their lives.

As a marketer, you can no longer force people to pay attention. Buying television ads or calling people at home is no guarantee that people will listen to what you have to say. This is why permission marketing is so effective—you reach people who have a worldview that the messages you promise to send them are a valuable part of their lives.

This fortress of attention is not impervious, of course. People still notice things they didn't intend to see. They get caught up in fads, notice unusual commercials, can't help but pay attention to something that's happening just down the street. But these are random interruptions, not the sort of predictable, scalable effects that marketers can depend on.

BIAS

My friend Lisa wrote a best seller a few years ago, and reading the reviews on Amazon is an astonishing experience. About half of the readers gave the book five stars. They talked about how poignant and well-written the book was. They mentioned that they had bought four or five copies for their friends. The other half? They gave it one star. They vilified Lisa, her writing, her lifestyle and even the people who liked the book.

What's going on here? How can one book generate such diametrically opposite points of view? Simple. The book didn't generate anything. All it did was give people a chance to express the biases they had before they even opened the book.

It's tempting to be a crusading marketer. To set out to turn coffee drinkers into tea drinkers, vodka drinkers into teetotalers, Republicans into Democrats. And every once in a while, you get lucky and succeed. But this is a difficult and challenging path.

People don't want to change their worldview. They like it, they embrace it and they want it to be reinforced.

VERNACULAR

Once you've presented a story to people who share your worldview and are paying attention, the vernacular you use becomes astonishingly important. The words, colors, typefaces, images, media, packaging, pricing—all the ways you can possibly color your story—become far more important than the story itself.

I'm writing this as I sit in the Dragonfly coffeehouse in Pleasantville, New York. The vernacular is perfect for the story they intend to tell. Elvis (the early Elvis) is on the stereo. The stone statues of Buddha are in the window and the ceramic mugs make just the right sound as they touch the surface of the stone tables. The blackboards are hand-written and a guide dog in training is sitting under the table, softly whining.

The coffee and tea (the "products" ostensibly sold here) are identical to that for sale at half the price across the street at the diner. But that's okay, because no one is here for the product. We're here for the story and the way believing it makes us feel.

This is why copywriting and Web design and photography are so important. Why it matters how your sales force dresses and speaks. When Pat Holt strings together a list of words not to overuse—"Actually, totally, absolutely, completely, continually, constantly, continuously, literally, really, unfortunately, ironically, incredibly, hopefully, finally"—she's not being a stickler for formality and grammar. Instead she's reminding us that words matter, that poor word use is just a red flag for someone who wants to ignore you.

GEORGE CARLIN

While any author would jump at the chance to include something from George Carlin in a book, I actually have a good reason: euphemisms.

Euphemisms may seem like political correctness run amok, but they are actually focused on telling stories that are framed to get past a person's biases and give the speaker a chance to tell a story. Here are ten from Carlin, some pretty facetious:

> prostitute = commercial sex worker
> nonbelievers = the unchurched
> lying on a job application = résumé enhancement
> police clubs = batons
> porn star = adult entertainer

    room service = private dining
    nightclub = party space
    fat lady = big woman
    committee = task force
    maid = room attendant

In each case, the euphemism allows the person telling the story to paint a picture before the door of attention gets slammed in her face. No one wants to be on a committee, even if it's a good one. *Committee* creates a knee jerk, a quick decision about stasis and boredom. *Task force* (at least for now) has enough energy to it to allow us to listen to the rest of the sentence.

Same is true with *nightclub*. No one is going to book a bar mitzvah, no matter how edgy, at a nightclub. But a *party space*—at least we'll take a look before we turn it down.

EARLY ADOPTERS AND SO ON

Technology marketers love to talk about early adopters and the mass market. Early adopters are the techno geeks and nerds who go out and buy the latest gizmo. The mass market waits, sometimes for years, until a technology is much cheaper and totally proven. The DVD followed this path. It took about ten years to make its way from the geeks' living room to your mom's.

Well the difference between early adopters and the mass market is actually one of worldview with a different name. It's the same as the difference between people who are inclined to go to a doctor instead of staying home when they've got the flu. The same as the difference between people who are vegetarians and those that would rather have a steak for dinner.

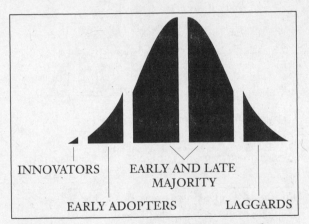

INNOVATORS   EARLY AND LATE MAJORITY

EARLY ADOPTERS   LAGGARDS

This curve shows the worldview of the audience for new technology devices. Folks on the left (a minority) will eagerly buy just about anything that's new. The mass market is in the center. On the right are people still having trouble programming their VCR.

Geoffrey Moore studied how products move through the product adoption (early adopter and so on) curve in *Crossing the Chasm*. A big part of succeeding with stories is realizing that so many categories work the same way. The mistake is to assume that there's only one product adoption life cycle curve, that the only worldview that matters is a person's likelihood to accept a new technology. This is just one tiny flavor of worldview, even though the math and the concepts are the same.

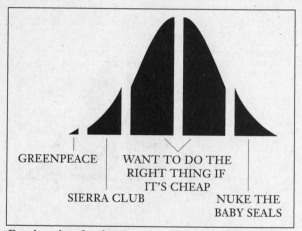

GREENPEACE WANT TO DO THE
RIGHT THING IF
IT'S CHEAP

SIERRA CLUB   NUKE THE
                               BABY SEALS

For the sake of making a point, here's the same curve as it applies to the U.S. population and its worldview when it comes to environmental issues.

Over and over, marketers focus at the center of every curve they encounter. And every time, they're disappointed. The center is crowded, jammed with noise and devoid of unfilled wants. It's at the edges that you'll find people with an unfulfilled worldview.

IT'S ACTUALLY SMALLER THAN THE WORLD

I worry about using the term *world*view. It implies that a consumer's bias affects the way he thinks about big things—world-sized issues. In fact, more often than not, worldview affects the way we approach tiny issues. It affects the way consumers think about chocolate bars or résumés or a commercial on the radio. **A worldview is the lens used to look at every decision a person is asked to make.**

At the same time, it's naive to believe that a million people have a million different worldviews. Instead, worldviews are clumpy. There are common memes that group strangers together. I'm not the first to describe some of these similarities, but the essential message here isn't that any particular clump is important in and of itself. Instead, I'm hoping you'll get the knack for finding the clumps. Doorbells in New Hampshire and health-food stores actually have a lot in common.

THERE ARE NO DOORBELLS IN NEW HAMPSHIRE

My family and I went swing-state canvassing last year, and we discovered that (at least on the block we were assigned) no one had a doorbell. Big houses and little houses—all the same. Obviously, doorbell technology has been around a while, so these New Hampshire residents could have had a doorbell if they wanted one.

The reason that there are no doorbells? It's a symptom of a neighborhood worldview that is a bias against strangers. If you're a friend, come on in. If you're a stranger, go away. Not surprisingly, understanding this worldview is essential if you're intending to sell much of anything in this neighborhood. The vernacular of presentation (ringing doorbells) was not only a waste—it was actually counterproductive.

FINDING THE TOOTH FAIRY

Tom's of Maine stumbled on to a great example of story-telling.

From a marketer's perspective, toothpaste is a challenging purchase. People don't buy it very often and the brand selected doesn't matter very much to most people. The cost is so low that it's irrelevant, and few consumers are walking around wishing they could find a better-performing toothpaste. As a result, not many people notice ads or promotions for toothpaste, unless they're clipping coupons to save money.

So Tom told a story. A story about health food and responsible manufacturing and authenticity and voting with your toothbrush. The story fit perfectly into the worldview of a tiny portion of the audience. By selling the toothpaste only through health-food stores, Tom was talking to a group of retailers (and ultimately consumers) that agreed with the way he framed his story and were happy to hear it.

Over time, as Tom's of Maine was found in more and more homes, the word started to leak out. They crossed the chasm from health nuts to everyone else. One user would tell a friend, then another. Soon people who wouldn't ordinarily have sought out a special kind of toothpaste were believing the lie and sharing it with others. Not because it did anything for their teeth. Because it made them feel good.

Here's what Tom did. He:

> found a shared worldview;
> framed a story around that view;
> made it easy for the story to spread;
> created a new market, which he owns.

A WORLDVIEW IS NOT A COMMUNITY

By definition communities share (some) worldviews. The community of soccer moms in my town, for example, have similar (but not identical) biases about everything from politics to automobiles. That's pretty obvious. What makes them a community is that they talk to each other. They share ideas and adjust their biases and choices based on what other members of the community do. When the first soccer mom bought a minivan, it started a buzz, a buzz that spread through the community as each mom considered the story behind this new kind of car.

But a shared worldview doesn't make a community! Individuals who don't like car salesmen, for example, aren't part of a coherent community. They just share a bias: they don't talk to each other because they're not particularly interested in the other people who also hate car dealers.

In this book, I've decided to occasionally use the word community instead of market. That's because I think the best marketing goes on when you talk to a group that shares a worldview and also talks about it—a community.

WHERE TO FIND THE NEXT KILLER WORLDVIEW

I have no idea.

I could tell you that it's progressives in Alabama or high-fidelity audio fanatics now interested in movies. It might be people who are open to messages about organic gasolines or plastics. Or perhaps you could marshal the growing backlash against technology that is difficult to use.

This is an art, not a science, and that's why it's so interesting (and profitable). While the answers aren't evident, the step you must take to find the answer is.

You must look for it.

Once you acknowledge that identifying a group that shares a worldview can dramatically change the outcome of your marketing, then you'll already be on the lookout for it. You won't obsess as much about manufacturing issues or marketing hype or spam. Instead, you'll seek out a story that will change the way you do business.

THE MOST IMPORTANT WORLDVIEW

(at least for our purposes)

The desire to do what the people we admire are doing is the glue that keeps our society together. It's the secret ingredient in every successful marketing venture as well.

You have no chance of successfully converting large numbers of people to your point of view if you try to do it directly. But if you rely on the nearly universal worldview that people like being in sync with their peers, you are likely to find that those who believe your story will work hard to share their lie with their peers. If your story is easy to spread, and if those you converted believe that it's worth spreading, it will.

The essential conclusion is that not all worldviews are created equal. People with worldviews that are private, that are embarrassing to share or that belong to people who don't like keeping up with the Joneses don't offer as high a yield to marketers as other, more profitable ones. The best worldviews from a marketer's point of view are those that include a healthy dose of "I gotta share this!"

As Rob Walker points out in the *New York Times*, all of the word of mouth in the world is the work of a small subset of the population. Call them thought leaders or bzzagents or sneezers or early adopters, this personality trait means that some consumers are worth far more than others to anyone interested in telling a story.

Not only will some people spread your story more than others but often they'll compete with each other to see who can do it more prominently. At the Robin Hood fund-raising dinners in New York, it's not unusual to see a Wall Street trader bid $700,000 for the right to bring six friends to the Victoria's Secret winter show.

In describing the large number of extremely wealthy art collectors at Art Basel Miami Beach, Amy Cappellazzo of Christie's said, "They'd prefer to spend $500,000 here or at auction on something they could buy privately for $50,000. These people are traders and they're incredibly savvy about markets." Actually, paying ten times as much to show off isn't savvy, it's stupid. Until you realize that what they're buying isn't the art, it's the process.

Lucy Mitchell-Innes, a prominent art dealer, told the *Times*, "People want [the art] because their friends do. If it's unique and there's only one, it's less appealing."

Not only the rich compete for the privilege of telling stories. We see precisely the same behavior in companies bidding up the price of domain names and consumers waiting in line to spend $1 on a yellow charity bracelet.

It doesn't matter if you're selling $3 socks at Kmart or $3,000,000 paintings in Miami. A lot of people want what everyone else is buying.

TWO MORE WORLDVIEWS WORTH MENTIONING

1. "If it ain't broke, don't fix it."

The reason so many effective solutions take forever to get implemented is that the fear of change is greater than the cost of sticking with what you've got. In other words, people wait until they have a heart attack or get diabetes before they go on a diet.

This is the most frustrating worldview a marketer can face. You believe in your product, you know your product will help people, but people refuse to notice it, never mind purchase it.

One solution is to reconfigure your offering so that it's easier to start using. Salesforce.com did this with sales automation software. Instead of offering a product that requires spending hundreds of thousands of dollars to fix something that isn't broken, Salesforce.com's salespeople get to offer the much smaller decision of buying a monthly service.

The other solution is to "break it." If your product (and by extension, your marketing) breaks an existing system, the consumer has no choice but to buy your solution—or at least to notice it and consider it. E-mail worked this way. Once your customers and coworkers had e-mail, you had to buy it as well because your previously satisfactory communications strategy (fax and so on) was now ineffective.

2. *"I like working with you."*

The reason that permission marketing and 1:1 marketing are so effective has nothing to do with the ethics of spam. Instead, these techniques work because they group together people with a similar worldview. The people you're talking to now are the prospects and customers that have a bias to work with you.

When someone opts in to get e-mail from Dailycandy .com, she's making a clear statement about her worldview. That gives a site a leg up in communicating with their customers, because they're able to frame their messages in a way that gets it heard.

What are you doing to reward people who have a worldview like this? How can you help them spread the word that it's a good worldview to have?

PUTTING FRAMES TO WORK

Imagine that your boss has charged you with introducing a new kind of salty snack food, a chip of some sort.

In the old model, you'd identify a target market, find media that reached that market, create some advertising and run it. You'd pay slotting allowances and get your bags of chips (in brightly colored packages) into the chip aisle. Perhaps you'd run some coupons.

Starting from a worldview model, you'd approach it differently.

Understanding that the chip aisle of the supermarket is jammed (as is your target consumer's ability to pay attention), you can start over by identifying a segment that might notice a new story, told in a different way. In this case, let's choose moms that believe "salty snacks aren't healthy and my kids don't eat them."

This mom doesn't go down the snack food aisle at the supermarket. She doesn't notice advertisements for snack foods either. She seems a poor prospect for this product, but if you can tell the right story, the market is yours for the taking.

So you design the story. The chips will be made from soy, not potatoes. They will be non-GMO, organic, low-fat and salted with a little sea salt and dulse, for flavor, not sodium. The chips will come in a box, not a bag, and you won't sell them in the snack aisle at all:

instead, you'll pay to have them slotted in the produce department.

Now you're telling a very different story. You're using frames to match the worldview of the segment you're trying to reach. And if you do it right, there's an excellent chance they'll notice the change in the environment and will give your story a try. If the chips are good (and assuage mom's slight guilt over depriving her kids of chips!) then you've made a convert.

And no, moms with this worldview aren't a cohesive community. But moms are still moms, and moms talk to each other. Your target moms will start serving the chips at birthday parties and sending them into school with lunches. They might even mention how much their kids like the chips at the next neighborhood get-together. So the story spreads. Pretty soon people who don't share their worldview will be seeking out the chips. Soon after that you'll be able to move the chips to the snack aisle, because you've shared your story and your audience will follow.

> **Step 1: Every consumer has a worldview that affects the product you want to sell. That worldview alters the way they interpret everything you say and do. Frame your story in terms of that worldview, and it will be heard.**

STEP 2:
PEOPLE NOTICE
ONLY THE NEW AND
THEN MAKE A GUESS

It's impossible to transmit every single fact, instantly, to every person you want to reach. So marketers tell stories. Sometimes we tell stories with packaging or with advertising or with words. Sometimes we tell a story with a smile, or with a sign in front of a building. Often those stories are well intentioned and even an attempt at communicating all the facts. But when a human being eventually confronts the idea, he will interpret it in his own way—he will lie to himself, creating a judgment without access to all the facts. The best marketing techniques, then, are the simple stories that are the most likely to break through, the most likely to be understood and the most likely to spread. And because the rules keep changing, the tactics must change as well.

I'm amazed to find myself writing this, but the purpose of this book is to persuade you to be *less* rational. Stop trying to find the formula that will instantly make your idea into a winner. Instead of being scientists, the best marketers are artists. They realize that whatever is being sold (a religion, a candidate, a widget, a service) is being purchased because it creates an emotional want, not because it fills a simple need. Marketers win when they understand the common threads that all successful stories share.

In the legendary words of Judy Garland, "Hey kids! Let's put on a show."

HOW YOUR BRAIN WORKS

If you want to tell a great story, you need to know about the brain that's going to hear that story.

Whether you create a product, market a service or run a nonprofit, you win when you spread your ideas. If your idea spreads from person to person, you'll grow in influence and everything will get easier. I call an idea that spreads an ideavirus. If everyone who matters knows your idea, you win.

Ideas are worthless without a place to live. An idea in a book or on a whiteboard has no impact. Just like a virus, an idea needs a host, a brain, to live in.

A virus spreads through a community by jumping from host to host. When the scientists at the Centers for Disease Control try to understand a biological virus, they must first understand how the host (that's you and me) interacts with the virus.

The same thing goes for an ideavirus. But instead of tracking how the body reacts to a germ, we need to understand how our brain responds to the ideas and inputs we encounter.

Recent research on brain function has focused on four ways we're able to deal with the significant amount of information we process each day:

LOOK FOR A DIFFERENCE

When we encounter something for the first time, we compare it to the status quo. If it's not new, we ignore it.

LOOK FOR CAUSATION (COINCIDENCE)

Once we decide to pay attention to something, our brain sets to work to figure out how it happened. If a window breaks, we want to see the golf ball on the floor. We instantly make up a rule or a theory about how this thing came to occur.

USE OUR PREDICTION MACHINE

Then we make a prediction. We predict what will happen next in our world. If our prediction is right, then the external surprises will cease and our brain can settle back in and start ignoring things again.

RELY ON COGNITIVE DISSONANCE

Once we've made up our mind, once we've got some assumptions about causation and we've made some predictions, then we stick with them. We ignore contrary data for as long as we can get away with it and focus on the events we agree with.

LOOK FOR A DIFFERENCE: THE FROG AND THE FLY

A bullfrog's brain weighs about twenty-four grams. A human's? About sixty times as much. A garden-variety small frog might have a brain weighing as little as ten grams. Clearly humans have a significant brainpower advantage over tree frogs.

A surprisingly large chunk of your brain is reserved for your ability to use your eyes and to take action on what you see. Seeing is difficult and responding quickly to what you just saw takes a disproportionate amount of brain tissue.

Despite the substantial evolutionary investment in human brainpower, despite the vast number of brain cells devoted to our eyes and our ability to process what we see, most people are unable to snatch a housefly out of midair, with or without their tongue. The fly is too fast and we are too slow.

Yet frogs do this every day.

How does a frog get by with so little? How can a frog, with its minuscule brain, find a fly, track it, aim its tongue, launch it and then capture the fly in less than a second?

The frog has optimized its brain for hunting flies. It turns out that a frog is unable to see anything that is motionless. A frog surrounded by recently killed bugs will starve to death, unaware that there is plenty of nutrition just inches away. At the same time, a frog can grab a fly out of the air with its tongue far faster than any person can.

The frog's secret? It watches only for changes in the environment. It has a brain that can only do one thing well, and that's watch the sky for moving bugs. By ignoring the static environment and only focusing on what's new, it can be far more efficient than a human when it comes to catching flies.

Humans use the same strategy far more often than we realize. Not to catch flies, of course, but to keep up with the huge influx of data we wrestle with every day. Have you ever caught your car odometer flipping from 999 to 1,000? You may not remember ever having looked at your odometer before, but somehow, by strange coincidence, you catch it during the big change. Obviously it's not a coincidence at all.

We're constantly scanning the world around us for changes. Walk into your house and within a heartbeat you know if something has changed. You glance at your watch a dozen times in a row without consciously knowing what time it is—until you discover that you're late for something, and then the data jumps to the forefront of your awareness.

Yes, we're just like frogs. We notice changes most of all. No, we can't grab a fly, but we can tell at a glance if there's a new brand of beer at the market or if the mailman got a haircut.

LOOK FOR CAUSATION: BROKEN IPODS

Everything happens for a reason, doesn't it? Even if you don't consciously agree with that statement, your brain sure does.

The ability to refine our superstitions is one of the brain's greatest talents. Unlike virtually any other living being (or even most computers), humans insist on finding a theory to explain what happens to them.

The *New York Times* recently ran an article about otherwise intelligent, rational people who were sure that the shuffle feature on their iPod was broken. The shuffle feature is supposed to randomly select songs and play them. These users knew for certain that something was wrong because their iPods appeared to keep playing certain songs over and over. Instead of being random, it appeared to these users that the iPod was favoring some songs over others.

A quick look at the song count on my iPod confirmed that this is exactly what happens—some songs are played ten times as often as others. But that's the way it's *supposed* to be. That's the way randomness works. Random doesn't mean perfectly even. Far from it.

These superstitious iPod owners, though, had made a decision about what their player liked (and what it didn't like). They gave the machine a personality. Whenever a particular song came up again, they made a mental note of it. "Aha! See, it does love Fatboy Slim. There he is again." Of course, they were just as quick to ignore those instances when a rarely played song came up.

That's why we're afraid to walk under ladders and why we believe that a rabbit's foot can bring us good luck. We make a guess about what works, and focus our attention on how often we're right (and forget how often we're wrong).

In November 2004 Diana Duyser posted a grilled cheese sandwich for sale on eBay. If you look at a photo of the sandwich in just the right way, your mind may play tricks on you and you will see the face of the Virgin Mary burned into the Wonder Bread. More than 200,000 people visited her page on eBay and the sandwich sold for about $28,000. Please remember that this is a ten-year-old grilled cheese sandwich! One person asked me if it was a fake. A fake? A fake what? Is that as opposed to a grilled cheese sandwich in which the face of the Virgin Mary is actually, really and truly there? Earnest brain cells invented the face because our brain is always inventing a plot, a story, an explanation for what we see.

We need to see explanations where there are none because our brains are too restless to live with randomness. **In the face of random behavior, people make up their own lies.**

USE YOUR PREDICTION MACHINE: MAKE A GUESS

t's amznly esy to red wrds tht ar mssng mst of th lttrs.

Presented with data, we struggle mightily until we have a theory about what's going on. We fill in the blanks and make a guess about what we're seeing. Once we're satisfied that the guess is pretty good, we can relax. You might have had no trouble decoding the first paragraph of this section, but when you try to read *Tre iuall nwa ou etts iht*, you probably give up in frustration. It's annoying when our guessing strategy doesn't work. We like to be able to guess and we want our guess to be right. More often than not, that guess is heavily influenced by our worldview.

COGNITIVE DISSONANCE: PRESIDENTS WE HATE

Consider three presidents: Kennedy, Nixon and Clinton. No doubt you have strong opinions about all three. Almost certainly, you either love or hate each of these guys.

But all three had very mixed tenures in office. All three did great, heroic deeds, and all three did things that are embarrassing or that hurt the United States. It's hard to hold contradictory ideas in our heads, isn't it?

Because of an event or even their physical appearance, you made an assumption about each of these men. And then as more data trickled in, you used stories that supported your view to reinforce it (Nixon not only was a crook, he lied about Vietnam!) and ignored the stories that contradicted your vision.

Research shows that consumers of goods and services act in precisely the same way. Switch the contents of a Coke can and a Pepsi can and then do a taste test. Odds are that people will prefer the brand long before they prefer the contents. This gets metaphysical, so hang on: they'll pick the Coke can (with the Pepsi inside) as their preferred drink even if they like Coke more. We drink the can, not the beverage. That's because we'll do whatever we can to prove our initial assertion right.

If you're a marketer, this is bad news and good news. Good news for the Harvard grad interviewing with a hiring attorney who also went to Harvard: even if the applicant is a yutz, the bias of the interviewer is in her favor. Bad news for the gate attendant at an airline that has an employee who just mistreated a passenger on the phone or at curbside.

WE GET WHAT WE EXPECT

Diners at the Union Square Café in Manhattan rave about the service. The service at this restaurant is fine, but it's raved about because that's what diners have persuaded themselves is the truth—even before they sit down. All the good moments are remembered and commented upon, while the lapses are forgiven.

We get what we expect because what we get is just a story in our heads. We expect something to occur and our brains make it so.

Armed with this data, it's easy to set out to trick people into believing something is new and different when it's not. It's easy to sell a story that just isn't accurate. And as we'll see in a bit, there's no easier way to crash and burn. Authenticity is more important than getting noticed.

> Step 2: People only notice stuff that's new and different. And the moment they notice something new, they start making guesses about what to expect next.

STEP 3:
FIRST IMPRESSIONS
START THE STORY

Here's what we know: almost every important buying decision is made instantaneously. These snap decisions affect everything we do, and we'll bend over backward to defend them later.

YOU DON'T GET MUCH TIME TO TELL A STORY

As we saw in the section about the workings of the brain, people can't function without a story. Humans are incapable of properly sorting every fact presented to them. Instead, consumers make up a theory about what's going on and then work hard to refine that theory.

The amazing thing is how quickly these stories get invented. People decide about a retailer or an industrial salesperson or a book cover or a television show in a matter of seconds. It's a particularly devastating process when it comes to evaluating another human being.

TAKE A LOOK AT THIS PICTURE

It represents just a fraction of an entire animal. And yet looking at just a tiny piece of it, you had no trouble imagining the trunk, the tusks, the huge feet and even the odor of the elephant. We make instant judgments because they help us deal with the outside world.

Try this one:

All you see is parts of three letters. But the typeface is enough to tell you at a glance what to expect inside the store. Not just what sort of coffee, but the kind of chairs, the attitude of the people behind the counter and the sound the espresso machine makes. You could probably identify the store blindfolded.

The thing is you've never ever seen *this* elephant before, you've never been inside *that* Starbucks before, but you're still willing and able to make a huge number of predictions based on a snap judgment and a tiny amount of data.

THE FIRST SNAPSHOT

In Malcolm Gladwell's brilliant book *Blink*, he proves conclusively that humans make decisions on almost no data—and then stick with those decisions regardless of information that might prove them wrong. We decide that a politician is just like us, and it doesn't matter a lot when he misspeaks, makes poor decisions or even gets indicted. We've already made up our minds and we're going to look at everything that happens through the rose-colored glasses we put on after that first meeting.

In one study Gladwell recounts, we discover that the decision to sue a surgeon for malpractice has nothing whatsoever to do with whether or not the doctor was negligent or careless—and everything to do with whether he was pleasant to deal with in the few minutes the patient was with him in the examination room. In other words, we decide *before the surgery* whether we'll sue if anything goes wrong.

While the magnitude of these judgments might surprise you, the overall message shouldn't. The only chance our ancestors had to survive in the jungle was to make accurate split-second assessments. If you needed a week or even a day to decide if another Neanderthal was friend or foe, you were pretty dead. We inherited the ability to make accurate snap judgments.

As creatures with egos, though, we need to defend our decisions. The boss doesn't like to admit she's wrong, and neither do we. So we skew our perceptions to match that first judgment.

If you've ever applied for a job (or been on the hiring side), you've seen this snap judgment phenomenon in action. The vast majority of job interviews are over in less than five minutes. Either you're hired and the rest of the interview is just a chance to confirm that decision, or you're not, and the rest of the interview is a courtesy to hide the fact that you didn't get the job after just a few moments of chatting.

That's why speed dating works. Sixty people show up at a bar. The women are organized into a circle of tables, and the men rotate, sitting with each prospect for about six minutes. Isn't this an unreasonable way to pick a companion for the evening, never mind a mate for life? Of course it is, but it accurately mimics the way we actually make decisions.

This is how embezzlers get to keep their jobs for so long. Why people stick with politicians who don't do what they said they were going to do. And why we're superstitious.

Turn on the radio and you can hear the political flaks and loudmouthed talk show hosts spinning, spinning, spinning: aggressively describing their opponents' actions as reprehensible and ignoring the fact that their guy did precisely the same thing—but worse. This isn't a new phenomenon—it's just part of the same snap judgment justification we've all been doing for millennia.

In order to survive the onslaught of choices, consumers make snap judgments. In a heartbeat, people take in the way a person looks and talks and smells and stands and dresses. They examine packaging and pricing and uniforms and lighting and location and the Muzak in the background and instantly come to a conclusion. Of course, there's data that contradicts this conclusion. That data is ignored.

The pieces of the story come together in an instant and the story is told. If the story is confusing or contradictory or impossible, the consumer panics and ignores it. But if the story is compelling and addresses basic desires like fear or power or acceptance, it might just be embraced.

Remember, though, that the story that gets told is dependent on the worldview the consumer brings to the table. Occasionally a product is so powerful it can change our worldview. But don't count on it.

THE MYTH OF THE FIRST IMPRESSION

After reading about our snap judgments, it's easy to fall victim to an obsession with making a perfect first impression. After all you never get a second chance to make that first impression. We've got to dress for success, make sure the front of the restaurant is carefully swept and answer the telephone on the first ring: that first snap judgment is crucial.

The problem with that analysis is this: 99 percent of the time, the first impression is really *no* impression.

You can spend a fortune on your advertising, but most people will ignore it. You can wear a $999 suit, but most people won't notice. You can invest in your signage, your uniforms, your location, your pricing, your phone staff, the smell of your lobby—and virtually every prospect who interacts with you will walk away with no recollection at all of what just happened.

The problem with first impressions isn't that they're not important (They are important! They're crucial!) but that we have no idea at all when that first impression is going to occur. Not the first contact, but the first impression.

That's why authenticity matters.

It doesn't really matter whether a story we tell to a consumer is completely factual. If it's a good story, if that story is framed in terms of his worldview, then he'll tell himself the story and believe in the lie. The reason authenticity matters is that we don't know which inputs the consumer will use to invent the story he tells himself.

If our sign is cool and our location is cool but our people and our products aren't, we're not telling a coherent story. Only when a business or organization (or person) is authentic can we be sure that the story that's being told is consistent enough to impact the maximum number of people.

So here's the deal:

1. Snap judgments are incredibly powerful.
2. Humans do everything they can to support those initial judgments.
3. They happen whether you want your prospects to make a quick judgment or not.
4. One of the ways people support snap judgments is by telling other people.
5. You never know *which* input is going to generate the first impression that matters.
6. Authentic organizations and people are far more likely to discover that the story they wish to tell is heard and believed and repeated.

Spending an inordinate amount of time and money on your sign or your jingle or your Web site is beside the point. It's *every* point of contact that matters. If you're not consistent and authentic, the timing of that first impression is too hard to predict to make it worth the journey. On the other hand, if you can cover all the possible impressions and allow the consumer to make them into a coherent story, you win.

WHY YOU NEED TO CARE ABOUT SUPERSTITION

Superstitions are nothing but incorrect theories based on snap judgments. Bad first impressions lead to stories that aren't accurate—superstitions we tell ourselves and believe in.

People are superstitious about whatever it is you're marketing. You can ignore that superstition or you can rail against it, but both strategies will cost you. The alternative is the only one that works: use personal interactions that are so extraordinary and so powerful that they cause people to tell themselves a different story instead.

If a consumer has a lousy telephone experience with a hotel reservations agent, his impulse will be to hate the service from every person he interacts with when he finally arrives at the hotel. The only solution? It's not expensive carpeting, lower rates or a better mattress. The only solution is a warm, personal interaction between an authentic and caring individual and your disgruntled customer.

Facts are not the most powerful antidote to superstition. Powerful, authentic personal interaction is. That's why candidates still need to shake hands and why retail outlets didn't disappear after the success of Amazon.

THE RECYCLING STORY

When some people discover that recycling doesn't really work as well as believed, they get very upset. The same people who drive SUVs or buy tuna in single-serving cans get angry when it's revealed that those blue recycling boxes are only a palliative, not a cure to our garbage problem.

It turns out that recycling doesn't save as much money and resources as most people expect. In fact, in many cases, it actually costs more than it saves. The cost of handling and sorting and processing all that trash is just too high, especially in very densely or very sparsely populated neighborhoods.

But it's just a few cans. Why should people get so upset? Why sign petitions and hold rallies and inundate the mayor's office with phone calls when the program is canceled?

People rebel because the facts about recycling are so opposed to the entrenched worldview. Recycling makes us feel good. It salves our guilty conscience. It makes us feel pure again. When you take recycling away from us, you're reminding us that believing a lie is not quite the same as understanding reality.

People in New York were outraged when the city canceled recycling. Thousands continued to save up their cans and bottles just because it was so morally difficult to throw them out.

The recycling lie was subtle, multifaceted and deeply seated. Exactly the sort of story you need to tell if you want to build a brand that lasts.

Step 3: Humans are able to make extremely sophisticated judgments in a fraction of a second. And once they've drawn that conclusion, they resist changing it.

STEP 4:
GREAT MARKETERS
TELL STORIES WE
BELIEVE

ARE YOU A MARKETER?

I think you are.

I think you have an idea you'd like to see spread. I think you'd like people to join your church, vote for your candidate, ask you out on a date or even offer you a job.

If you've got employees, I bet you'd like them to do more of what you're hoping they'll do. If you're applying for a loan, I bet you're hoping you'll get it.

Every day all of us market. Some of us are really lousy at it, and worse, believe the reason for our failure is some sort of intrinsic inadequacy. It's not. You're just not good at telling stories. Yet.

WHY DID YOU BUY THIS BOOK?

What a weird business. People buy books (millions of them every year) without knowing what's inside. In fact, the only way people know for sure if they're going to like a book is to read that book, at which point it is unnecessary to actually buy a copy.

It's not just books, of course. People buy a car or a stove or a house after just a cursory run-through. We vote for a presidential candidate without saying, "Why not run the country for a month and then we'll see . . ."

Consumers pretend that they're rational and careful and thoughtful about the stuff they buy. Actually they're not. Instead they rely on stories.

Stories matter.

If you bought this book, it's not because you'd already read it and liked it.

You probably bought it because you'd read something else by the author . . .

> Or it was recommended by a coworker . . .
> Or you read the back cover and figured it was worth a shuttle flight . . .
> Or it was face out on the bookshelf and something about it caught your eye . . .
> Or because the clerk glanced at you with awe and respect when you picked it up . . .

There are hundreds of reasons, and not one of them has to do with your firsthand experience in actually using the product (the book).

You bought this book because of a story you were able to tell yourself. Some of the stories are fiction (does walking under a ladder actually curse you with bad luck?) while others are based on fact (a car with an EPA rated mileage of fifty miles per gallon is going to need fewer fill-ups).

Even if the story is based on fact, all the stories people rely on to make decisions are blown out of proportion. One story isn't the whole truth. Al Gore never said he invented the Internet and he's not prone to insane exaggeration, but it was a good story and it helped tens of thousands of people make up their mind about him. An SUV isn't a safer car than a station wagon, but the story the car tells sure makes us feel that way as the driver climbs on board and sits way up high. And that guy you hired in accounting, the trustworthy one with the firm handshake and the great references—you're not really certain he's not going to embezzle all your profits, but he looked you in the eye and it made you feel good to hire him, didn't it?

TELLING STORIES IN AN INTERNET WORLD

Marketers freaked out (and I use that term carefully) when the television-industrial complex came crumbling down. They panicked because they had been living and thriving under the illusion that marketing = advertising, and when advertising stopped working, they had no idea at all what to do.

P&G and other big advertisers spent millions trying to invent television-like commercials for the Web. (You can still find committees and commissions that lobby for this sort of thing within the Net community). Pretty quickly, though, they discovered that if people *could* skip the ads, they *would*.

In an Internet world, opportunity for marketers has nothing to do with re-creating mass marketing and creating commercials that can't be skipped. Instead marketers can use the many dimensions of our media culture to tell more complex stories faster and more effectively than they ever could have using television commercials.

Now we know that marketing = storytelling, and everything an organization does supports the story. So *everyone* is in the marketing department and a company either tells a story that people care about, or their story disappears.

HOW TO GET ELECTED PRESIDENT

The brutal election of 2004 is a great case study. There are three good reasons:

1. It's an event that people around the world are familiar with.
2. Hundreds of millions of dollars were spent, but some of the best successes (and worst failures) were absolutely free.
3. There was a lot of storytelling going on.

Why did John Kerry lose against an incumbent with near-record-low approval ratings after spending more than $100,000,000 on his campaign? Simple. He didn't tell a coherent story, a lie worth remembering, a story worth sharing.

People make decisions big and small based on just one thing: the lie we tell ourselves about what we're about to do. And Kerry failed to tell a story we wanted to believe. No, not a story in a speech, but *living* a story, consistently telling us the story in everything he did and said. From the clothes a politician wears, to his spouse and his appointees, he's telling a story. Candidates sometimes want to manage response with a press release or a speech. It won't work anymore. Like him or not, George W. Bush did an extraordinary job of living the story of the strong, certain, infallible leader. John Kerry tried to win on intellect and he lost because too few voters chose to believe a story they perceived as inconsistent and unclear.

Like any competitive marketplace, the market for votes is filled with consumers who have already committed to a worldview, who have a bias in favor of their current choice and are delighted to ignore or even denigrate alternative brands. The temptation in politics is to be so certain of the facts of your case that you arrogantly believe you can persuade people to change their minds.

But voters, like all consumers, hate to admit they're wrong. The only way to change minds is to somehow get past the filters and safeguards that people erect to insulate themselves from opposing points of view—and then to tell a story that spreads. And in today's political climate, those stories are far more expensive than they ever were before.

Advice to the candidates for 2008: understand that half the voting population has a worldview that will cause a traditional partisan story to be ignored. Hillary Clinton, more than others, has a worldview problem because the vast majority of the electorate has already told itself a story about her. Same thing is true for John Ashcroft. He has no chance to tell his story to a large portion of the electorate—the worldview it holds about him has already been set. Conventional political wisdom says that either candidate, with a good enough organization and enough money, has a shot. I don't buy it. I believe that there isn't enough money in circulation to persuade those voters that have already made up their minds to change them.

If you start a campaign unable to speak to the people who need to hear your message, you've lost before you even begin—and the only way Ashcroft or Clinton can win is by persuading millions of people to change their minds. As we've seen, that's practically impossible for something as trivial as a brand of cosmetics. For a politician, it's inconceivable.

POSTCONSUMPTION CONSUMERS

Stories only work because consumers buy what they don't need. When a person really needs something (food, water, shelter) he cares a great deal about the essence of the purchase. If he's really hungry, the food is more important than the package. But being really hungry in our society is (fortunately) pretty rare.

Today the world is richer than it has ever been before. Even poor people in this country own a color television set. As a result, most everyone has what she needs (with the exception of medicine).

Alyssa is buying bottled water. Not because she's thirsty. Thirst can be quenched for free anywhere in the United States. What she *wants* is convenience or peace of mind or the satisfaction of knowing that she's got water from Fiji or Tanzania in her hand. She buys bottled water because she wants it, not because she needs it.

If consumers have everything they need, there's nothing left to buy except stuff that they want. And the reason they buy stuff they want is *because of the way it makes them feel.*

This occurs just as often with products sold to businesses. The myth of product superiority in business-to-business products is just that. The people who buy for business are people first, and they buy things that get them promoted, that make them feel safe and secure or that give them a sense of belonging. The battle between Salesforce.com and Seibel is a great example. Even though Salesforce.com has a significantly better software-on-demand product (by any measure), Seibel continues to make sales of their inferior competitive product. Ingersoll-Rand bought Seibel's product because they were in the middle of a crisis and couldn't take the time to try an alternative. The reason people stick with Seibel is simple: if you've been a Siebel customer for a decade, it's far easier to justify the decision to stick with that company to your boss. And that's what you're buying—not software, but the justification, the story.

Consumers care a lot about the buying process. They care a lot about packaging and peer approval and the out-of-the-box new product experience. They care about the provenance of the item and the circumstances under which it was made. Sure, once something is purchased, people care about durability but they care far more about the way the staff at the company treats them when it breaks.

Is there a connection between the utility of a product

or service and the way it makes a person feel? Of course! A consumer shapes his desires based on what he's heard about its utility from other people. He is excited to see a movie because the reviewer said it was good. He wants to buy a Dodge Viper because of the acceleration or he wants to hire an accountant from Deloitte because the firm helped another company so dramatically. Consumers are not so fashion conscious that all utility is irrelevant.

But is the utility of the product the main way people shape their desires? No way! And that, in two words, is why you need the ideas in this book. In almost every meeting I go to, people are desperate to understand why their product or service isn't selling better. They always begin by pointing out how good their product is, how much better/faster/more durable it is. They are obsessed with the utility and they can't understand why the market isn't responding to their microanalysis of the difference between their offering and that of their competitor.

We don't need what you sell, friend.

We buy what we want.

> Step 4: Stories let us lie to ourselves. And those lies satisfy our desires. It's the story, not the good or the service you actually sell, that pleases the consumer.

EXAMPLES: STORIES FRAMED AROUND WORLDVIEWS

There are more worldviews than I count, but here are a few, together with descriptions of how successful marketers told stories to people with these biases.

"I BELIEVE A HOME-COOKED MEAL IS BETTER FOR MY FAMILY"

So how can a marketer possibly grow a supermarket brand?

There are twenty thousand new products introduced to supermarkets every year, struggling for just a few hundred slots on the shelves. The competition spends billions on advertising. Most new products are boring, me-too imitations that aren't worth a second look. It's a brutal marketplace for anyone trying to make a safe, standard, traditional offering.

The folks at Banquet decided to tell a story instead.

They found an audience with a worldview that matched a product they had the ability to talk about. It turns out that millions of Americans feel guilty about the fact that they no longer cook dinner for their families. They were raised to believe that a home-cooked meal = love = family = healthy and in our modern world, they can't find the time or the energy to pull it off.

A lot of these people own Crock-Pots, the electric slow-cooking device used for making soups and stews. John Hanson of Banquet introduced Crock-Pot Classics, saying, "Banquet Crock-Pot Classics contain all of the high-quality ingredients needed for a slow-cooked meal—like tender meats, fresh vegetables, hearty potatoes and perfectly seasoned sauces—and are ready to cook with less than five minutes of preparation. At the end of the day, Banquet Crock-Pot Classics welcome home families with the inviting aromas of a slow-cooked meal." In other words (if Banquet had stated the real deal): "Here's a bunch of stuff, preserved by chemicals and freezing. Dump it all in the pot, turn it on and you'll end up with something we could have just as easily precooked for you and sold frozen, ready for the microwave."

ConAgra, which markets Banquet, has a home run on its hands. Test market sales were 250 percent higher than average. This is a high-profit, high-sales item that will succeed for years and years.

Of course, ConAgra isn't telling the whole truth, when

it claims that there's no difference between dumping the bag into the Crock-Pot and buying something to go at the local restaurant. Actually, there is a difference because Crock-Pot Classics contains "thiamine mononitrate, modified food starch, yeast extract, salt, hydrolyzed soy protein, sugar, monosodium glutamate, propylene glycol, caramel color, disodium inosinate, disodium guanylate, soy lecithin, salted California Chablis wine, high fructose corn syrup, anchovies, corn protein, and emuslifier."

It doesn't matter. The lie the consumer tells herself is what matters. It's a lie about the way the house smells when her family walks in, a lie about doing the dishes, about not throwing out piles of to-go boxes. It's the way the product makes her feel when she sees her family sit down and eat together.

ConAgra succeeded because they didn't try to make a product for everyone and because they told a story, not the facts.

"I BELIEVE SHOPPING FOR LINGERIE MAKES ME FEEL PRETTY"

A good friend is thinking about starting a small lingerie shop aimed at women with high household incomes. Our conversations about the store fit right into this thinking about stories and lies.

I imagine that a few years ago, the nascent shopkeeper

would have talked about price points and inventory. She'd have worried about monthly cash flow and rental expenses. After that, a discussion of a convenient location would have followed.

These are all commodity-focused issues. The old conceit of a retailer was that if you offered the right products at a fair price in a convenient location, you'd do fine if you watched your expenses.

Today, the issues are totally different. The world of lingerie is just a click away. Everything, from anywhere in the world, at the best price is online in just five seconds. So if you're going to start a traditional retail outlet, you better have a better reason than "filling a need."

The issues we discussed about her shop: What's the story? What will people get out of a visit? Who will they meet while they're in the store? Should I serve herbal tea or espresso? I need to have half as much inventory as the standard store—but which half?

If someone leaves the store feeling better than when she arrived, my friend has successfully told a story. The consumer will tell herself a lie—a lie about how a few ounces of fabric can make her feel sexy, perhaps. And that lie will spread, guaranteeing the store a loyal (and profitable) following.

So growth starts with better questions. Questions about storytelling, not about commodities.

"I DON'T BELIEVE MARKETERS"*

There's a huge cohort of consumers that shares the worldview that marketers are lying scum. If you, the marketer, say it, the consumer won't believe it. If you brag about having the best service in town, these people won't believe you. If you claim that you have the best prices or the highest scores in one survey or another, they'll ignore you.

Subtlety matters.

If you choose to tell a story that's more subtle, something more interesting and more believable, these people will choose to pay attention. Once you've got their attention, there's your chance. If you actually deliver the best service in town, you've given this audience the tools they need to spread your service story.

You don't get to just sit down and make up a story and expect that people will believe it merely because you want them to.

Consumers are too clever for that.

You can't claim your workmen's comp insurance agency has the best service and expect that the lie will strike a chord. You can't insist that shopping at your store is fun and expect that people will rush on over just to experience it.

*And I read the fine print.

This is a hard lesson for a lot of marketers to learn. It's easy to tout your features, focus on the benefits, give proof that you are, in fact, the best solution to a problem. But proof doesn't make the sale. Of course, *you* believe the proof, but your audience doesn't. The very fact that you presented the proof makes it suspect. If a consumer figures something out or discovers it on her own, she's a thousand times more likely to believe it than if it's just something you claim.

This is where the art of marketing occurs. For most products and services, skywriting, billboards and telemarketing are precisely the wrong ways to spread a message. Not because they won't be noticed—they probably will. But because they won't be believed.

In order to be believed, you must present enough of a change that the consumer chooses to notice it. **But then you have to tell a story, not give a lecture.** You have to hint at the facts, not announce them. You cannot prove your way into a sale—you gain a customer when the *customer* proves to herself that you're a good choice.

The process of *discovery* is more powerful than being told the right answer—because of course there is no right answer, and because even if there were, the consumer wouldn't believe you!

"I BELIEVE SUSHI TASTES BETTER IF THE CHEF IS JAPANESE"

Does it change things when you discover that Becks Light and St. Pauli Girl beer are made on the very same assembly line? Why does the sushi at Masa ($300 per person for dinner) taste so much better than the $40 sushi down the street? Maybe it's the extraordinary wooden bar that gets sanded after every meal or the attention paid to you by a very talented chef.

Expectations are the engine of our perceptions. And complex stories carry all sorts of perceptions. Where people choose to shop, the way the transaction is handled, the noise, the music, the lighting—each element is at least as important as the item itself.

Ralph Lauren generates a huge portion of its sales from seconds and job lots sold at the many Polo factory stores around the country. There are so many of these stores (and the demand is so high) that many of the items sold aren't seconds at all. They're designed and produced for the factory stores. People tell themselves a story about finding a bargain, they build up the expectation by driving thirty miles out of their way (while on vacation, no less) and then are delighted to spend $40 for a $400 jacket that was never intended to be sold for $400 and probably cost $4 to make.

"I LIKE BOOKS SETH GODIN WRITES"

I didn't write this book.

What I mean is that Seth Godin didn't write this book. It was written by a freelancer for hire named Mo Samuels. Godin hired me to write it based on a skimpy three-page outline.

Does that bum you out? Does it change the way you feel about the ideas in this book? Does the fact that Seth paid me $10,000 and kept the rest of the advance money make the book less valuable?

Why should it matter who wrote a book? The words don't change, after all. Yet I'm betting that you care a lot that someone named Mo wrote this book instead of the guy on the dust jacket. In fact, you're probably pretty angry.

Well, if you've made it this far, you realize that there is no Mo Samuels and in fact, I was pulling your leg. I (Seth Godin) wrote every word of this book. And I apologize for fooling around with you. But the point should be pretty obvious. One of the reasons that the ideas in my books spread is that readers expect that they'll be spreadable. You expect that what I write will be fun and useful and pretty irreverent. Once you hear that the book was written by someone you've never heard of, it's a totally different story, isn't it?

The ideas are the same but the lie is different. And the lie is at least as important as the ideas inside.

"I LIKE TO BEAT THE SYSTEM"

In the 1980s a few innovative entrepreneurs came up with a great business. They bought some brand-name stereo speakers at a great discount (last year's model) and packed them into a rented U-Haul truck.

Then they parked the truck behind a dorm at Harvard and started whispering, "Pssst. . . Hey! You wanna buy some speakers?" While they never actually said that the speakers were stolen, it was pretty obvious to passersby that they were. Harvard students shouldn't have fallen for this. Of course, they did. In droves.

The entrepreneurs sold out the (not-really-stolen) speakers in no time. The story the students told themselves made the purchase incredibly appealing, even if the speakers were priced higher than they would have been down the street at Tweeter, the local stereo store.

Tweeter spent plenty of money on advertising and real estate. These entrepreneurs made it easy for people to tell themselves a story. Who won?

"AMAZON HAS THE BEST CUSTOMER SERVICE"

Why does Amazon continue to earn the highest scores on the American Customer Satisfaction Index? (The index is the definitive benchmark of how buyers feel about what business is selling them.)

Because their customers expect they will.

They expect the service at Amazon will be terrific (because it was the last time) and so they give them the benefit of the doubt. Good outcomes are remembered because they support the customers' worldview. Bad outcomes are forgotten, written off as random events.

Amazon worked hard, harder than almost any company in history, to provide amazing service. They so exceeded expectations that their customers started to tell themselves a story about Amazon. As a result, it's now easier, not harder, for Amazon to maintain its amazing reputation. People believe it because they want to believe it.

"ORGANIC FOOD IS BETTER"

Organic Style magazine is a publishing success story. But why does style need to be organic? Why does organic need to be in style? Why is this the fastest growing segment of the food industry, creating markets not just for food but also for soaps, clothes and other consumables?

I was checking out at the supermarket last week and smiled when I saw what the woman in front of me was buying. She was just like me, even though we didn't have one item in common in our baskets.

My basket had organic olive oil, organic tomatoes, organic tofu, organic goat cheese, Scharffen Berger chocolate and vacuum-sealed white beans from France. Hers had two Amy's organic frozen dinners, hormone-free chicken breasts and two bags of Pirate's Booty cheese snacks. She also had organic shampoo and some organic toothpaste.

We'd both fallen for the story. We were telling ourselves a complex lie about food, the environment and taking care of our families.

Does organic food taste better than other foods grown with similar care? Not really.

Is organic food better for you? Well, it's not clear, but living near New York City introduces so many contaminants into your system that the point is certainly moot (it's said that running for half an hour along the FDR Drive on the East Side of New York is equivalent to smoking a few cigarettes).

Is buying organic food a cost-efficient way to support family farmers who respect the land? Not unless you buy it from a farm stand. Most of the money goes to marketers and processors, not the folks who work so hard to grow it.

So then what's going on here?

Organic food is a relatively cheap way to satisfy this consumer group's desire to take care of our families, to take care of our bodies, to take care of the Earth and to feel we're doing as much as we can to tread lightly. It's a way some Americans use to assuage our guilt about being the world's least efficient consumers of just about everything.

Not everyone buys organic food. Many people have a worldview diametrically opposed to what organic food represents. That doesn't change the fact that organic food is an extraordinarily good story. The hypersuccessful Whole Foods Market chain of supermarkets is based almost entirely on this story.

Whole Foods sells tons of potato chips, candies, saturated fats, sugar-loaded juices and more. All at inflated prices. But that's okay. It's okay because people don't shop there for food. They shop there because it makes them feel good. They buy foods they want, not need. And all of us derive satisfaction from believing we've done the right thing.

People don't want to know all the details about their food. They don't want to consider how the cow was slaughtered or how much gas it took to truck those grapefruit here or what those fats will do to their arteries. What people want is a story, a lie they can tell themselves and their friends.

Do I want everyone on Earth to buy organic foods, to eliminate many of the side effects of groundwater pollution and increase the taste and nutrition of what we eat? Of course I do. That's not the point. What matters is that organic food is selling well (retailers that sell organic are growing three times faster than traditional stores) because of the way buying it makes people feel, not because of what the food actually does.

That's why I pay Michael (the charming organic farmer at the Hastings Farmers' Market) $10 a pound for baby spinach. It makes me feel good to believe.

IMPORTANT ASIDE: FIBS AND FRAUDS

Did the stolen speakers on the truck story make you feel a little queasy? It seems vaguely unethical. Tricking people into buying speakers because they think they have been stolen is unethical, isn't it?

Well, marketing the $90 speaker cable that makes a stereo sound exactly the same as the $12 speaker cable in a blind test is just as unethical, isn't it?

People (marketers included!) believe, way down deep, that the right thing to do is to buy a product or service because of what it actually does. We are taught that we ought to make products and services that actually do something, instead of marketing things that we need to tell stories about. Our prospect's hard-earned money ought to be spent investing in things with plenty of utility, not in useless fads that will deliver very little value.

We say that's what we believe, but then we—along

with all the other consumers out there—buy overpriced designer T-shirts, eat at overpriced but trendy restaurants and stay in fancy hotels on business trips. How can we rationalize this?

The psychic impact of a nasty flight attendant is more important than a plane arriving ten minutes early at its destination. The enthusiasm a company's staff has when they install new robots on the factory floor can be just as important as the work those robots actually do. In other words, irrational beliefs aren't a distraction—they are an intrinsic part of the quality of the product.

Which leads us to the fibs and the frauds. Georg Riedel is a fibber—an honest liar. He's an honest liar because he tells his customers something that isn't true—his glasses make wine taste better—and then the very act of believing his lie makes the statement true. Because drinkers believe the wine tastes better, it does taste better.

Storytelling works when the story actually makes the product or service better.

It's pretty easy to tell a fibber when you see one. Fibs are lies that make the story come true. If I think that automating my factory will save me money, it's more likely to turn out that way. If I believe that a politician understands my needs, I'm more likely to give him the authority to actually make things happen. If I believe a stock is going to go up, and I share that story with my friends, the company is actually likely to rise in value.

Frauds are a little trickier—and more dangerous. A fraud is a marketing pitch that once revealed as a story makes a believer angry: it's deceitful. A fraud is a story that's told solely for the selfish benefit of the marketer. A fraud is marketing with side effects.

HI, IT'S DAVE!

Lennox is a company that makes furnaces and air filters. The company is more than a hundred years old. In the spirit of a family-owned business, their ads and their voice mail are hosted by Dave Lennox, company president. Give them a call at 1-800-4Lennox and you can hear for yourself.

"Hi! I'm Dave Lennox!"

Dave always talks in exclamation points.

Dave Lennox appears to be a good story. In a world of faceless corporations, the idea that a family-owned business where the owner—the grandchild of the founder—answers the phone is heartening.

Installing a Lennox furnace thus feels like a smart purchase. It makes the buyer feel safe and secure to know that a real person stands behind an important purchase. It makes it worth more.

Until the furnace breaks. Until the customer visits the Web site and picks up the phone to call Lennox.

I just discovered that Dave Lennox died more than

fifty years ago. That he's an actor. That there is no Dave Lennox. I felt tricked. Wouldn't you?

The problem isn't with the lie I believed. The lie actually made the process of buying the furnace enjoyable. The problem is that the story isn't authentic. The company doesn't follow up. Once you reach someone on the phone at Lennox, it's clear that not only is Dave long gone, but his spirit is gone as well.

A fib is a story that makes something better. It's a way of describing your offering (in all the ways humans describe things) that makes the thing itself more effective or enjoyable. Nobody really minds a fib, and if your consumers find out that your story isn't based on facts, they're not enraged.

A fraud, on the other hand, is a story based on little or nothing. It's a story you tell primarily for personal gain. And worst of all, a fraud, when discovered (and it will be discovered), enrages your consumer—probably forever.

FIBS ARE TRUE

Is a Mercedes really fifteen times better than a Toyota? After all they'll both get a driver from here to Cleveland in about the same amount of time. The Toyota will probably use a bit less gas and the Mercedes might even be twice as comfortable. But fifteen times better?

That depends.

When a car buyer slams the door of the Mercedes, it tells a story. A story about solidity and workmanship, a story about safety and performance. That doesn't happen with a Corolla. What's the Mercedes story worth? How does it make the buyer feel about the marketer and the brand and the way he's chosen to spend his money?

Mercedes spends almost all of the price premium they charge building stories for customers to believe, to enjoy and to share. They put those stories into the radio or the way the gas pedal feels or the intelligent actions of the windshield washers.

Mercedes wins because they are authentic in their quest for a car worth talking about. Cadillac fell apart when they stopped believing their own story—and focused on grabbing money instead of telling stories. Cadillac turned into a fraud, using the story of their brand and their history to trick people into buying a car they'd end up regretting. It took decades to fix that selfish mistake.

FRAUDS ARE INAUTHENTIC

Decades ago, when Nestlé contributed to the death (according to UNICEF) of more than a million babies, the company should have known they were telling a story that was a fraud—hoping that mothers would believe a deceitful story designed to trick most of them into buying and using a product that would actually make their lives worse.

In the developing world, for many women breast-feeding is healthier than bottle feeding. Nestlé can't make any money on breast-feeding, though, so they used the power of marketing to spread an idea: bottles are better.

Nestlé worked hard to tell that story. The story was simple and was framed to fit the worldview of many moms in the developing world: Western technology is better for your baby. That story encouraged mothers to stop breast-feeding and start using powdered Nestlé formula, which was provided free to many new moms.

If Nestlé had told an authentic story, one that was aimed at moms with AIDS or those who had trouble feeding a baby the traditional way, they could have built a long-term business. It would have been a smaller business, but it would have survived scrutiny and grown organically—by improving the lives of their customers.

The story Nestlé chose to tell didn't make things better, though. The positive aura of the Western technology story they framed did absolutely nothing to save the lives of babies who should have been breast-fed in the first place. This isn't a case of allowing people to lie to themselves in order to make the experience better or to encourage people to do something they'd end up being glad they did—it was about getting people to do something they'd be sorry they believed in.

Nestlé's powdered formula frequently got diluted by families unable to afford to buy as much formula as they needed. Unclean water was mixed into the powdered formula, and as a result many babies got sick.

Because the story wasn't accurate, because it was actually the opposite of the reality of the situation for most moms, the effect of a consumer lying to herself was devastating. Marketing is now so powerful that caveat emptor is no longer a valid defense. Nestlé learned a hard lesson and backed off, but the point applies to all marketers. **Just because people might believe your story doesn't give you a right to tell it!**

Could Nestlé have sold this story without the active participation of the consumers they were speaking to? No, of course not. The story only worked because of the worldview these consumers had before Nestlé even showed up. The consumers were complicit. It doesn't matter.

Marketers are wrong when they insist that "all we do is offer options—it's up to consumers to decide for themselves." Marketing is now so well developed and so embedded in our culture that consumers no longer make decisions based on a rational analysis of facts. Instead they decide based on the stories they're told. To disclaim responsibility for a fraud is cowardly.

I don't know if you can tell, but . . .

I'M ANGRY

I'm angry when babies are killed by deceitful marketers. I'm upset that politicians and corporations and even job seekers have figured out how to tell stories that trick people into doing things they regret later. I'm bitterly disappointed that something that could do so much good is often used to selfish ends.

It's not just the obvious stuff you've seen on *60 Minutes*. Somewhere along the way, marketing started walking down a slippery path of something worse than irresponsibility: nonresponsibility. It's okay to market knockoff LiveStrong bracelets because, hey, it's a free market. It's okay to puff your copy on your Web site or weasel your way around your no-spam privacy policy because, hey, you've got quarterly numbers to hit.

"Everyone does it" is not the excuse that will stop this slide—it exacerbates it. Until marketers start to take responsibility for the stories we tell and the promises we make, consumers will get increasingly more skeptical and suspicious—and all marketers will lose.

The good news is that even though marketing is far more powerful, it's now harder than ever to get away with a fraud for long. The millions on the Internet are watching the reactions people have to your stories. Google is tracking your behavior. It's almost impossible to keep a tangled story straight. The only robust, predictable strategy is a simple one: to be authentic. To do what you say you're going to do. To live the lie, fully and completely.

KEEPING PROMISES

Deceitful marketers prey on a consumer's inability to tell fibs from frauds. They create a fashion but then don't deliver on their promises.

The danger of writing this book is that it will enable and embolden the deceitful storytellers. It could make selfish marketers who are interested in a quick buck even more successful—because if they tell a good story, they're more likely to succeed. The good news is that this group is in the minority. Even better, once consumers are able to see the effect that stories have on them, they'll be in a much better position to believe the good ones and avoid the bad.

A LIE WON'T WORK FOR LONG IF IT'S REALLY A LIE

If you must calculate your story, pulling some miracles out of the air, that means you probably can't live the story. Georg Riedel wouldn't succeed with his wine glasses if his entire organization didn't believe the lie the consumers believe. The best coin dealers own their own coins for investment, just as George Gilder, the fabled technology prognosticator, lost more money than most of his readers when the telecommunications bubble tanked.

Yes, you need a story. No, it may not be inauthentic.

TELLING THE HONEST FROM THE NOT-SO-HONEST

It's in the eye of the beholder. It's not up to me or to the pope or the ethicists. Your story fails when the person who believed it decides it fails.

You and I know that magicians aren't really magical. When we discover that a magician is doing a trick, we don't get angry. You also know that makeup doesn't really make women look twenty years younger and that your favorite restaurant doesn't have a kitchen as clean as your kitchen at home. That's okay. You buy into these lies because both you and the storyteller benefit as long as you believe.

But what happens when we discover that Beech-Nut apple juice for toddlers was systematically watered down? What happens when an author like Robert Allen starts spamming people in order to make a few more bucks? When we recognize the fraud for what it is, we feel incredibly stupid. Something more than our bank accounts is damaged—our egos are damaged. As a result, it's almost impossible for the marketer to regain our trust.

TRUTH AND BEAUTY

Am I telling you not to worry about quality? To ignore the essence of your product, the way it works, the way you develop it, the impact it has—all so you can tell a story?

For the last decade, I've been writing about treating consumers with respect, about transparency and about creating things worth talking about. Now all of sudden, it appears as though you're supposed to throw that away and pander to the lowest common denominator.

Far from it.

Doing the right thing pays off. Storytellers who trick consumers get caught. They become inconsistent and sooner or later, they get punished. Wonder Bread filed for bankruptcy because the American public realized that eating too much white bread and Twinkies was killing us. Countless computer companies that promised consumers more than they could deliver have disappeared. Brands get rich, then cut corners and get hammered.

I was clear about this in *Purple Cow* and I'll repeat myself here: if you want to grow, make something worth talking about. Not the hype, not the ads, but the thing. If your idea is good, it'll spread.

The public demands that you tell them a story. The story is part of the product or service that they buy—in many cases, the story is what people set out to buy. But at the core of a story is the thing, the real thing, the essence of what you've built. And if you try to build on a rotten core, you'll succeed for a bit but then you'll lose.

THE CIGARETTE PREFERRED BY DOCTORS!

Philip Morris killed millions of people by marketing an extraordinarily addictive product to those not yet addicted. Beech-Nut lied about putting water into apple juice. McDonald's teaches millions of people to eat a certain way and to create a huge amount of waste (in creating the food and packaging it as well) as a result of their marketing. Sure, it's just storytelling, but marketing that succeeds turns into the lie we tell ourselves—and that hurts us and the people around us.

It comes down to authenticity. Telling a story that won't disappoint, that you believe and that your customers will have no trouble living with.

Marketing isn't the problem. Marketing is just a tool. **People are the problem.** People with short-term pressures and greedy, selfish goals. But it's not just the people in marketing who are responsible. Consumers are complicit as well. When they refuse to spend a few minutes understanding side effects and buy a story instead, consumers aren't acting as adults, they're just pawns. But when I see how some marketers misuse their sophisticated tools, trading long-term health and benefits to large populations in exchange for a few dollars, it makes me embarrassed to be a marketer.

> The good news is clear: authentic marketing, from one human to another, is extremely powerful.
> Telling a story authentically, creating a product or service that actually does what you say it will leads to a different sort of endgame. The marketer wins and so do her customers.
> A story that works combined with authenticity and minimized side effects builds a brand (and a business) for the ages.

WHY SOPHISTICATED WOMEN HATE MINIVANS

My wife won't drive one. Neither will our friend the *New York Times* columnist who lives down the street from us.

Hey—it's a car, not a lifestyle statement. It's transportation, not a branding tool or a personal marketing choice. It's the most expensive discretionary expense in people's lives, but most people rarely choose a car for a logical reason.

Every car tells a story, and a minivan tells that story particularly clearly. It doesn't matter that minivans are durable and cost-effective and fuel-efficient and way more comfortable than SUVs. What matters most of all is the way it makes someone feel. The story (soccer mom driving a taxi for kids all day) demolishes the utility of the car itself. Avoiding this story costs hundreds of thousands of dollars to people over a lifetime of car buying.

Instead of buying the car that makes sense, more people choose to buy an SUV. They believe the story, not the facts. SUVs get lousy mileage. They are more dangerous to the driver, to her passengers and to people in other vehicles than minivans. They create more than their share of pollution. They create more wear and tear on the roads and take up extra space on parking lots and highways. But they make people feel good.

Is there something wrong with this? Is it a sign of weakness or foolishness when we believe a story instead of looking at the facts?

I don't think so—until we consider the side effects.

Marketing is so powerful today that marketers have a new kind of responsibility. A responsibility to *both* long-term profits and to the long-term viability of their markets. If you make a fortune but end up killing people and needlessly draining our shared resources, that's neither ethically nor commercially smart, is it? Nuclear weapons have killed a tiny fraction of the number of people that unethical marketing has. It's time we realized that there may be no more powerful weapon on Earth.

Marketing stories can have a nearly instant impact, and that impact can be felt for decades. Paul Prudhomme created a story about redfish that made the fish a staple in restaurants around the country—and came very close to causing its extinction. Coke and Pepsi created a story about corn syrup, and this myth is causing the premature death from heart disease and diabetes of millions of people.

I refuse to accept that there's a difference between a factory manager dumping sludge in the Hudson River (poisoning everyone downstream) and a marketing manager making up a story that ends up causing similar side effects. Marketing is an awesomely powerful tool, and marketers share the same responsibilities everyone else does.

"We're just serving the market," "We're satisfying people's needs" and "Adults should have the right to make a decision about this" are the words of a weasel. Crafting a story that tricks people into making short-term decisions that they regret in the long run is the worst kind of marketing sin. Refusing to take responsibility for it afterward is just cowardice.

Just because you want to make more money is no justification for using the power of lying to hurt the rest of us.

WHO'S YOUR NANNY?

I'm not proposing that marketers become the conscience for our society. If we try to one-up one another in the do-gooding category, it'll never end (and nobody will make any money). Sure, the world would be better if everyone rode a bicycle to work, but that doesn't mean you shouldn't market cars.

I'm proposing a simple test for separating the honest stories from the deceitful ones. It revolves around two questions the consumer should ask the marketer:

"If I knew what you know, would I choose to buy what you sell?"

and

"After I've used this and experienced it, will I be glad I believed the story or will I feel ripped off?"

SUVs don't pass my test. Nor do some sorts of life insurance. On the other hand, overpriced consulting may very well be an example of a good sort of story.

In the long run, the "good" stories pay off for marketers. Not just in sleeping well at night, but in building a business or an organization that truly thrives. In the long run, good stories create a virtuous cycle, in which consumers benefit and profit enough to buy even more—in a market that can last for the long term.

THE GULF OF TONKIN

In 1964 Lyndon Johnson had a marketing problem. He and his top advisers were concerned about Southeast Asia and wanted to commit more troops there. But they didn't have a story they could easily tell to the voters or to Congress.

So Johnson made up a story about unprovoked attacks on U.S. ships in the Gulf of Tonkin. His administration said that the ships *Maddox* and *C. Turner Joy* had been attacked by North Vietnamese torpedo boats. On the weight of this story, Johnson persuaded Senator Fulbright of Arkansas to lead the fight for a resolution in Congress—and Fulbright got eighty-eight out of ninety Senate votes and every single vote in the House for a resolution giving the administration the authority to use as many troops and weapons as it chose to in Vietnam. To vote against the resolution was to take the risk of being seen as wishy washy or even unpatriotic. (The two senators who voted no were not reelected.)

The administration told us a story, and we believed the lie. It fit the worldview of many voters in the United States—to use force when under threat or attack. Johnson framed the story beautifully. How could a senator vote against our national interests? How could he vote with the enemy? Either you're with us or you're against us, went the worldview.

There are two facts that belie this strategy as a successful marketing approach, however. The first was that Johnson and McNamara and the rest of the team worked ceaselessly to hide the side effects from Congress and the American people. Rather than telling a story that we'd be glad we believed once we understood all the facts, the administration concealed the long-term and horrific side effects of their war.

The second fact was that the original story was a total fabrication. There was no attack on those two ships. If you want to use a modern euphemism, it was "faulty intelligence." Once the Pentagon Papers revealed how Johnson had misled us in creating the very core of the story, support for the story started to fade. The story changed and our support went with it.

I don't care what your politics are—if you're a talented marketer, you can see the problems here. The story a marketer uses *must* be a good one, a story based on some version of reality. **Belief in the lie must not ultimately harm the consumer because if it does, you'll run out of consumers and credibility far too soon.**

THE EMPEROR ACTUALLY LOOKED GOOD

We all grew up with the tale of the emperor who was hoodwinked into believing that he had bought beautiful clothes from two swindlers. He was taken in by a story—if you couldn't see the clothes, you were stupid. The emperor bullied the populace into believing that only smart people could see how well dressed he was and, of course, the villagers cooperated by reminding one another (loudly) how handsome the new outfits were. Only one brave child had the guts (and naïveté) to out the emperor and reveal that he was actually naked.

What's missing from the children's fairy tale is the fact that many of the villagers actually thought the emperor looked pretty good.

Sure, at first the typical villager was pretty skeptical (the emperor was naked, after all). But once enough people told him the story of the magical clothes, he began to believe it. As the word spread through the village, everyone began to believe.

Because they *wanted* to believe the story, they persuaded themselves that the emperor looked good. That's why the kid who finally spoke up and said, "Hey, the emperor is naked!" wasn't particularly popular. By telling the truth, he made his neighbors feel stupid and angry.

Telling people that they've believed a lie for a long time is no way to make friends. If it's a good lie, a lie that led people to enjoy themselves or to be productive, then taking that lie away is actually hurtful. I hesitated to write a book about lies, just because we love these lies so much.

If a friend has responded beautifully to a placebo drug, is it right to tell her that she's taking nothing but sugar pills?

If a person in Cuba is finding solace and meaning by attending the local Santeria religious ceremonies, is it right to point out that it's nothing but superstition?

If a dieter enjoys buying diet books (about 10 percent of all *USA Today* best sellers are on this topic) should we tell him that dieting actually leads to weight gain?

In an age of tremendous scientific advances and rational thought, it's ironic that superstition and religion and vivid stories actually drive us. Ironic but not surprising. As humans we've been trained since birth to make quick decisions, to be superstitious and tell ourselves the lies we learn by listening to stories.

Here's the thing: six months before this book was published, people were already criticizing my thesis online. It doesn't sit right. It feels like cheating, not like a legitimate way to succeed. Odds are, either you or someone you know is unsettled by the idea of telling stories.

We'd like to believe that efficient, useful, cost-effective products and services are the way to succeed. That hard work is its own reward. Most marketers carry around a worldview that describes themselves as innovators, not storytellers.

A lot of the people who buy marketing books are also people who have a worldview that says, "Tell me the truth, I don't want to hear a story." Alas, this group is small indeed. Members of this group don't want to hear my story about stories.

But, hey, storytelling isn't *my* idea. It's the idea of your customers.

It's your customers who want to be told stories. It's your prospects who will walk away if you obsess about the sixth sigma of this or that without bothering to tell a story about it.

So please, don't hate me. Hate them.

STEP 5:
MARKETERS WITH
AUTHENTICITY THRIVE

CHANGING THE STORY REQUIRES PERSONAL INTERACTION

You don't get to make up the story. The story happens with or without you. If you're not happy with the story, the only way to change it is with direct contact between your consumer and a person.

That person might be the consumer's neighbor or friend or teacher or boss. Or it might be one of your employees.

Personal interaction cuts through all the filters. Personal interaction is the way human beings actually make big decisions—by looking people in the eye, by experiencing them firsthand. That's why it was so hard for the dot-coms to build a loyal following—they couldn't afford to provide the interactions that are built into the retail experience.

Personal interaction comes from allowing people to be people, not script readers. When a customer talks to a telemarketer reading a script from a cubicle in New Delhi or Omaha, there's no interaction. When a clerk tells the consumer, "That's all I can do, that's our policy," he's creating a negative interaction. But when a human being works with the consumer and takes independent action on her behalf, something changes.

Allowing your employees to post an honest blog or to engage in direct instant-messaging conversations with your customers is a way to promote honest communication. If it makes you nervous to do that, maybe you need to worry about authenticity a little more.

Sometimes the interactions are nasty or rushed or even selfish. But when they're genuine, they have an impact.

BEFORE I TELL SOMEONE A STORY, I TELL THAT STORY TO MYSELF

The goal of every marketer is to create a purple cow, a product or experience so remarkable that people feel compelled to talk about it. Remarkable goods and services help ideas spread—not hype-filled advertising.

The challenge lies in figuring out what's remarkable and actually making the remarkable happen. I believe the best way to do that is to craft a story that someone enjoys telling to himself. Before we are able to share a story with friends, colleagues or the Internet, we need to tell it to ourselves.

Politicians call these talking points. Retailers call it an experience. If you can build your entire organization around delivering a particular story, you've dramatically increased the chances that this story will actually get told.

EVERY PICTURE TELLS A STORY

If you're authentic, then all the details will line up. Your menu will match your food, which will seamlessly integrate with your staff and your decor. If you commit to a story and live that story, the contradictions will disappear.

If you want to send a message of friendly service, it helps to hire friendly people. If great design is at the heart of the story you're telling, you need a designer to run things and a designer to be your accountant as well.

I'm not letting you off the hook by encouraging you to tell stories. In fact, stories only *magnify* the need to have something remarkable (and honest) to say.

Humans are too smart to be fooled by a Potemkin village, a facade that pretends to be one thing and turns out to be another. Sure, you can fool some people once or twice, but this is the key lesson of the new marketing: **once fooled, a person will never repeat your story to someone else.**

If you are not authentic, you will get the benefit of just one sale, not a hundred. The cost of your deception is just too high.

EVERY CAR TELLS A STORY

Aston Martin has the new hot $150,000 car of the moment. The *New York Times* gave it a twelve on a scale of one to ten. You can also buy exotic cars from Jaguar, Volvo and Range Rover. And every one of them is made by Ford—and you shouldn't be surprised to discover that they even share parts.

Why doesn't everyone just drive a used Honda? If the purpose of a car is to get drivers reliably from point A to point B, then the overpriced and hardly reliable Jaguar is not necessarily a rational choice, is it? If a car is the single most expensive discretionary purchase most people make, and a car is the product that consumes the most resources and interacts with the largest number of innocent bystanders, you'd think people would choose a car fairly carefully.

In fact, almost every car that's bought is bought because of a story.

The best stories, though, are the authentic ones. The Lotus Elise has a long waiting list because in addition to looking cool, the car has a racing heritage and a corporate point of view that matches the story. The buyer doesn't have to worry about finding the Lotus brand name on cheap luggage at Costco.

The Toyota Prius tells a very different story. People choose this car in order to show the world how smart they are (even if they're not that smart). Toyota didn't just offer a car with great (fifty miles per gallon) gas mileage. The Prius engineers told a much more authentic story. They went further than they had to. Even the keys are smart.

When you approach the Prius, don't take the keys out of your pocket. The car knows you've got them and will unlock itself as soon as you touch the door handle. Get in and press the start button and drive away. Drivers get just as much joy out of the key system as they do from the mileage. And anyone who experiences the car (at a friend's house or the dealership) is told the "smart car" story in a way that seems far more authentic than gimmicky.

First Toyota chose to tell a story. Then the engineers built that story into the car.

THE AUTHENTICITY OF THE SOY LUCK CLUB

My number-one hangout in New York is a hard-to-find little coffee shop run by Vivian Cheng. The Soy Luck Club has fast, free Internet access, organic oatmeal cookies, soy shakes and really good tea. They've got comfortable chairs, a great staff and just the right sort of atmosphere.

Most people on the street walk right on by and don't even notice the club. A few, though, pause, take a quick look at the menu and the layout and the sort of people inside and then walk in as though they own the place. They've figured out—almost instantly—that this is their sort of place. The frame of Vivian's story matches their worldview and they're sold before they even order anything.

How does she do it? I know Vivian well enough to tell you that it's not an intentional gambit on her part. The luscious pressed whole-wheat bagels with banana and soy butter aren't on the menu because she's trying to trick someone into thinking the place is healthy and funky. The bagels are there because Vivian likes them and is proud to serve them.

The Soy Luck Club is authentic in every way because it reflects who Vivian is and what sort of place she'd like to hang out in. So how does she grow?

She could try to grow by persuading people who don't care about her particular style of ambience and healthy foods and fluffy couches that this place is *better* than Starbucks. She could grow by persuading people to eat more soy so they don't have a heart attack. Neither approach stands a chance of working. **People don't want to change their minds.**

Instead, Vivian is growing by reaching out to communities that will choose to pay attention, to individuals who have a worldview that will embrace the story she's trying to tell. Vivian framed her story in a way that matches that worldview. A block away, the Equinox health club gives out discount cards to the Soy Luck Club. The assumption (a correct one) is that people notice a discount card if it's given to them by someone they trust. Even better, people who pay good money to work out in the middle of the winter are significantly more likely to want to believe in a story of healthy nutrition right around the corner. So it grows.

Of course, Vivian will really have a home run once her loyal customers start telling stories to their friends— friends who might not share the worldview but are eager to do something that others are doing, eager to hang out at a place beloved by their best friends. That's how Starbucks succeeded and how the Soy Luck Club will as well.

FAKING IT WITH ICE CREAM

Cold Stone Creamery started with a powerful story and grew to nearly one thousand stores. Now, though, the story is getting confused.

Started about twenty years ago in Arizona, Cold Stone has storytelling at its heart. Here's part of their mission statement:

Say good-bye to frozen predictability and hello to a whole new way to experience dessert. But can you really go wrong when making people happy is your number one priority? At Cold Stone Creamery, our company's mission is to put smiles on people's faces by delivering the Ultimate Ice Cream Experience®.

They get it! They understand that people pay five or ten times the price of supermarket ice cream because of the way the experience makes them feel, not because of the ice cream itself. Families go to their scoop shops because of the story the experience tells them.

And Cold Stone has legions of fans. They have stores in forty-six states and people will drive ten or twenty miles out of their way to visit one.

The problem is that now they are focused on growth, and they're growing by franchising the business. Some of the local owners aren't as passionate as the founders, and the inevitable outcome is that the story is no longer authentic, which makes it hard to believe the lie.

Scoopers at Cold Stone Creamery occasionally break into song. They'll sing for tips and they'll sing about the joy of ice cream. At my neighborhood Cold Stone, though, they don't sing. They sort of whine a funeral dirge. It's obvious that someone ordered them to sing, and they don't understand why and they certainly don't care.

By hiring the cheapest staff they can find, it appears to me as though some of the franchisees are viewing their business as putting ice cream in a cone. It's not. They are in the business of telling a story. And the song and the smiles and the staff are a much bigger part of that than the ice cream. Cold Stone cannot cost reduce their way to success, because soon the hordes will stop coming when they find that the experience leaves them hollow. If the scoopers aren't having a great time, why should the customers? **Some senses count for more than others, but every sense matters.**

- the way a home smells when you visit an open house
- the clicking sound a cell phone makes when you dial it
- the location within a strip mall when you choose a restaurant
- the display in the window
- the way the receptionist answers the phone
- the typeface on the flyer
- the identity of the person calling you on the phone soliciting a donation

It's worth stopping for a second to understand how significant a change we're now dealing with. Just twenty years ago, what mattered was how well you crammed your idea into a sixty-second television commercial.

Things like price and retail distribution were the essence of your marketing strategy.

Today, whether you're an architect, an evangelist or a cookie marketer, the rules are very different. You win when you manage to make your story coherent. If you are able to live the story you want to tell, the people you're telling it to are more likely to believe it because you'll get all the details right.

When they put Silk in the refrigerated section of your supermarket (it doesn't need refrigeration), they were telling you a subtle story about freshness. When they put sports nutrition bars at the checkout instead of next to the vitamins, they are telling you a story as well. Tiny cues that deliver big messages.

IT'S THE *COMBINATION* OF SENSES THAT NOW CONVINCES THE SKEPTICAL CONSUMER

No sense works all by itself. You might be able to trick me with a handwritten menu in the window of your restaurant, but if the chairs are wrong (or worse, if the restaurant smells wrong), I'll bolt. You may be the best psychiatrist in town, but you won't succeed if the words you use in the first ten seconds of our first phone call have more to do with signing me up as a patient than your training does.

Early on in this book, I told you that marketing has become an art. The essence of that art is your ability to use nonverbal techniques to make me a series of promises (promises you intend to keep). Some people are fortunate in that they're able to generate these signals without realizing it. Most of us, though, need to do it on purpose. We need to work hard to understand what the biases of our prospects are and which totems we can use to tell a story to these people.

The best place to start? Copy someone in a different industry who's telling a similar story. Discover the cues and signals she uses. Do them all, not just a few. Your story is a symphony, not a note.

ALL SUCCESSFUL STORIES ARE THE SAME

Remember, the best stories promise to fulfill the wishes of a consumer's worldview. They may offer:

- a shortcut
- a miracle
- money
- social success
- safety
- ego
- fun

- pleasure
- belonging

They can also play on fear—by promising to avoid the opposite of all the things above.

Consumers are all different, but ultimately they all want the same outcome. They want to be promoted, to be popular, to be healthy, wealthy and wise. They want to be pleasantly surprised and honestly flattered.

This is standard marketing stuff with a new spin. Except it's not. **Because successful stories *never* offer the things marketers are most likely to feature:** very good quality. A slightly better price. The best you can get under the circumstances. A decent commodity at a decent price. Convenience. Nice people. A quality brochure. Few defects. Industry-standard warranty. None of these attributes are story-worthy. Not only aren't consumers going to tell themselves a story about these features, but they're certainly not going to think it's remarkable enough to share with their friends.

Almost nobody wants a better drill bit or a slightly more nutritious muffin. Delivering a remarkable story isn't easy, but it's worth it.

So the place to start with your product, your service, your organization and your résumé is this: what classic story can I tell?

COMPETING IN THE LYING WORLD

ONE STORY PER CUSTOMER

The principles behind creative storytelling are compelling, but what do you do when you have competition? How do you respond to competing stories in the marketplace?

The most important principle is this: you cannot succeed if you try to tell your competition's story better than they can.

It's almost impossible to out-yell someone with the same story. Years ago I gave a presentation to the Wal-Mart Internet team. They gave me a tour of their offices, which featured a huge banner that read "You can't out-Amazon Amazon." At the time, Wal-Mart was more than one hundred times bigger than their smaller competitor in Seattle. If Wal-Mart was afraid to go after Amazon, what chance do you have against your entrenched competition?

This is the most difficult competitive lesson to learn. Marketers (and all human beings) are well trained to follow the leader. The natural instinct is to figure out what's working for the competition and then try to outdo it. To be cheaper than your competitor who competes on price, or faster than the competitor who competes on speed.

The problem is that once a consumer has bought someone else's story and believes that lie, persuading the consumer to switch is the same as persuading him to admit he was wrong. And people hate admitting that they're wrong.

Instead, you must tell a *different* story and persuade those listening that your story is more important than the story they currently believe. If your competition is faster, you must be cheaper. If they sell the story of health, you must sell the story of convenience. Not just the positioning x/y axis sort of "we are cheaper" claim, but a real story that is completely different from the story that's already being told.

Woot.com is a modern Internet success story, with tens of thousands of subscribers and millions of dollars in annual sales. And yet woot doesn't advertise and has just a few dedicated employees. How did they do it?

Woot only sells one item a day.

They are not trying to out-Amazon Amazon. Instead, they tell a very compelling story and that story is easy to believe and easy to spread. Every day starting at midnight, they offer exactly one product at a great discount. When it's gone, that's it. Come back tomorrow and see what's new.

Woot is a purple cow. It's a remarkable business with a story that's easy to tell. And because the story is theirs and theirs alone, they have plenty of room to grow.

FLIP-FLOP

The facts are beyond dispute: George W. Bush was as much of a flip-flopper as John Kerry. But Bush told the story first. He and his team did a masterly job of telling a story about Kerry and his inability to stick with one story. Millions believed the lie.

The Kerry team responded with a doomed effort to point out that Bush flip-flopped as much as Kerry did. Of course, this story couldn't take hold because the other story was already in place. It didn't matter one bit whether the Kerry team's story was true or not. The competition was already having success selling this story, and so Kerry's people had no chance to succeed with it.

Then the Kerry campaign tried to make the case that flip-flopping was a *good* thing, that it was another word for flexibility. A hard story to tell because the flip-flopping story told by the Bush team framed Kerry in a way that matched the worldview of millions of people. In order to adopt Kerry's story, people would have to admit that they were wrong—and that almost never happens.

The best strategy would have been to go first. Failing that, the appropriate response would have to been to tell a completely different story, one that used a frame that matched the worldview of the undecided voter.

FINDING THE RIGHT COMMUNITY

Most often you're charged with competing with someone who has already succeeded with a story that's taken hold. (It's easier for investors and bosses to spend time and money going after a proven market, even though proven markets are the hardest to break into.) The competition's story has already spread through a community that shares a worldview, and your boss wants you to reach that same community with your story—she figures all you've got to do is frame it.

For example, you might be trying to raise money for your nonprofit from high-net-worth donors. Or you might want to sell season tickets to rabid sports fans. As we've seen, either campaign is awfully difficult. The good news is that the community you're targeting has already demonstrated how responsive it is to stories like this. The bad news is that they no longer need a new story. They've solved their problem and the best you can hope for is some scraps from the uninformed, not a big win.

The best alternative strategy is to find a different community, with a different worldview that wants to hear a different story. This matches the classic case of 7-Up described in *Positioning* (selling the UnCola to people who didn't want to buy Coke) but it goes far deeper than that.

I'm asking you to invent an entirely new story that is framed around the worldview of an underserved community. The WNBA did a pretty good job of this with women's basketball (I don't think their ultimate failure makes the case study less interesting—they failed because the big television money sports teams depend on never materialized). Instead of saying, "Hey, basketball fans, this is just like men's basketball, but the tickets are cheaper," the WNBA went to a new group (families and women and kids) and offered a fundamentally different story, with a changed standard for interactions between players and fans and a game experience that was contrary to the NBA's.

Is it guaranteed that you'll find a new community that will embrace you and make your success certain? Of course not. But it's also certain that addressing the community of your dominant competitor is going to fail.

SPLITTING THE COMMUNITY

What if you're entering a market where there is already successful competition and they've all bought your competition's story?

That means that your competition is already telling a story that's working. In order to grow, you can't tell the same story to the same people (even if you tell it louder or with more style). Instead you will find success by telling a *different* story to part of the community with a particular worldview that's different from that of the masses. For example, Masa, the $300-per-person sushi restaurant in New York, went to people who liked eating out and people who loved sushi and told them a different story: "This is the best sushi in the world, but only for people who are willing to pay for it."

Until the moment Masa showed up, there was a community of people who wanted to hear a story framed around sushi. This is convenient sushi or great sushi or a good value in sushi. This group was treated as a homogeneous group, sharing just one worldview: we like sushi.

Masa told a story to only part of that community. He told a story to people who in addition to the "I like sushi" worldview wanted to hear a story framed around "deluxe" and "best in the world."

Some people in the "I love sushi" community heard this story and believed it. It was framed with their worldview about food as well as their self-esteem and feelings about spending money. Other people said, "That's ridiculous." So by splitting the sushi worldview into two groups—the big group that believes sushi couldn't be worth that money and the smaller group that was willing and able to believe the story—Masa was able to peel off enough people to create a success. The restaurant will become a profitable institution only if the experience they've promised is actually delivered and remarkable enough that this new community starts bringing their friends.

While the worldview you are looking at may appear monolithic, it almost certainly is not. When the Fortune 500 started hiring vice presidents to spend their billions of dollars on information technology, it appeared that all five hundred of these chief information officers (CIOs) had the same worldview. Pretty soon, though, alert competitors discovered that some of them wanted to hear stories about avoiding risk, while others desperately wanted to make a name for themselves by appearing to be risk-taking mavericks. Companies like Broadview and IBM and Cisco carved up the market by working hard to discover who would believe which story.

THE OTHER WAY TO GROW

What if splitting the community doesn't get you a big enough share of the market? The other way to grow is to recognize that in every community, people have more than one worldview at a time.

Many people who spend good money on bicycles, for example, respond to stories framed around going fast. For a long time, this worldview was the core of the bike market. Italian companies like Campagnolo and some Japanese upstarts obsessed about telling an ever better story about speed.

Then a number of American companies (like Trek) started telling a different story to the same audience. It was a story about comfort. The comfort story persuaded people to spend $1,000 or $5,000 on a mountain bike or a hybrid bike that had a racing heritage (they were the original sponsor of Lance Armstrong) but was actually a pleasure to ride. It wasn't until 1990, fourteen years after they started selling racing bikes, that Trek took off. They did it by focusing on telling a story to the underserved worldview in the community of bike buyers. Today most of the successful companies in this market succeed by selling comfortable bikes to aging baby boomers. As bikers aged, their worldview changed and so did the successful stories. By relying on a story that was easier to tell and easier to take action on, they activated more people in the market.

REMARKABLE?
THE COW HAS NOT
LEFT THE BUILDING

INVISIBLE OR REMARKABLE?

In *Purple Cow*, I argued that safe was risky, that in a cluttered world, the only way to grow was to do something remarkable.

Now almost all the way through this book, I can hear you breathing a sigh of relief. "We can just tell a story!" It seems like an easy out. Figure out some internally approved story that you can trot out to the sales force and use in a magazine ad, and you're set.

Actually if you do that, you're dead.

You can't just use any story. You can't tell a selfish story from *your* point of view. You can't invent an inauthentic story or tell an amazing story when the reality is banal.

More than a thousand times since 2002, people have written to me and said, "We have a purple cow but we don't know how to get the word out." Guys, if you really have a purple cow (in the eyes of the consumer, not in the eyes of you or your board) you won't have any trouble at all getting the word out.

The only stories that work, the only stories with impact, the only stories that spread are the "I can't believe that!" stories. These are the stories that aren't just repeatable: these are the stories that demand to be repeated.

Your story doesn't have to be salacious or noisy or over the top. But it must be remarkable. Too often marketers are so self-absorbed that they believe that their story deserves to spread. Hey, you don't get to decide what spreads—the public does. Authentic stories that earn the right to be passed on will be passed on. It's up to you, the marketer, to earn that right.

THE REALLY AND TRULY GREAT NEWS

If you tell the right kind of story, you'll automatically become purple. All great stories are purple cows for one simple reason: a great story is believed and the lie is retold. Which means it's a remarkable story, which means you're a purple cow.

It's no accident that the marketers who understand how to tell stories consistently create purple cows. It's built into the process. My advice is to stop fighting your fear and just tell the best story you can imagine. The rest will take care of itself.

IN DEFENSE OF EXTREMISM

You're not the only one who wants to tell a story. As a result, your tepid, compromised approaches to storytelling—stories that will please everyone, even those who don't want to hear them—are likely to fail. The reason so many successful new offerings are run by non-compromising nutcases is that these true-blue storytellers refuse to compromise.

These people may be no fun to work for, but they have the ability to tell a coherent, consistent story that is the same from every angle. They're not faking it—they're living the story and those who want to hear it find that they understand the story loud and clear.

Consultants are all too often the bane of the story-teller's existence. Consultants get candidates to listen to polls and restaurateurs to change their menus. Instead of allowing yourself to be pushed toward the middle, you need to look in the mirror and realize that only a remarkable, authentic story is going to have a chance of spreading.

GOING TO THE EDGES: GETTING PEOPLE TO VOTE

Harvard economist Edward L. Glaeser did academic research that proves an obvious point: people on the edges are more likely to vote. Not the middle of the curve, but those who are incensed and focused and care deeply about only one issue.

This leads to predictable behavior from candidates. Get radical before the election to activate your likely voter base (notice that I didn't say "to activate the largest base"). Then after the election, move to the center where you can get more done.

The same thing is true for selling hot sauce or laser beams. Being remarkable, going to the edges, doing something worth talking about—these are all things that are rewarded with action by communities that care deeply. **You succeed by being an extremist in your storytelling, then gracefully moving your product or service to the middle so it becomes more palatable to audiences that are persuaded by their friends, not by you.**

GOING TO THE EDGES: THE TITLE OF THIS BOOK

If a story is what leads to a lie the consumer believes, why not call this book perhaps the more factually correct *All Marketers Tell Stories*?

I was trying to go to the edges. No one would hate a book called *All Marketers Tell Stories*. No one would disagree with it. No one would challenge me on it. *No one would talk about it.*

A talented marketer is someone who takes a story and expands it and sharpens it until it's not true anymore (yet). **Your goal should not (must not) be to create a story that is quick, involves no risks and is without controversy. Boredom will not help you grow.**

I believe the purple cow is at the heart of just about every business success story of the last decade. What I missed in that book was that the remarkable element must be part of a bigger story, a piece of cognitive dissonance that actually changes the way a consumer perceives what you make. And in order to do that, you must aggressively go to the edges and tell a story that no one else could tell.

WHEN STORYTELLING (AND THE COW) DOESN'T SEEM TO WORK VERY WELL

Big and small work fine. It's medium I worry about.

- *Small:* I think it's pretty easy to see how telling the right story can really help an individual. A résumé, a job interview, a date: in all of these cases, when the person you're dealing with has only a few moments to come to a conclusion about you, insisting on telling them just the facts is a sure way to fail. We get involved with people (at all sorts of levels) based on nothing more than a story.

- *Big:* It's also pretty easy to imagine how enabling consumers to believe the big lie works for an entire brand. A company like Dell or Nike thrives when people buy into a story that makes the service or product they offer work better.

- *Medium?* I get into trouble, though, in the middle. If you're launching a new kind of Totino's pizza (square, not round) or your database for nonprofits is now $100 a copy instead of $200, I think you're asking too much if you want fast growth. Sure, sometimes you hit a home run, but more often than not small changes get you small results. It's hard to be remarkable when you create artificial boundaries about what you can and cannot do in telling your story. It's hard to be remarkable when you and your organization insist on not changing the status quo.

One of my favorite little companies is called Little Miss Match. They sell more than 134 styles of socks for preteen girls. The cool thing is that customers can't buy a matched set. The company only sells socks that don't match (they don't clash, either). The story here is framed in terms of the preteen mind-set: these colorful, cool, mismatched socks will give a kid something to show her friends and will make her look really hip.

And the story works. Once a kid believes the lie, she's likely to show off her socks. And when she shows off her incredibly cool socks, she's hip. And the idea spreads. From one kid to another until it starts appealing to the kids who never had the "I want to be edgy" mind-set.

There are no small stories. Only small marketers. If your story is too small, it's not a story, it's just an annoying interruption. Kudos to Little Miss Match for taking a little product and turning it into a big story.

Make your story bigger and bigger until it's important enough to believe.

BONUS PART 1:
MASTER STORYTELLERS AND THOSE WHO ARE STILL TRYING

I WANT TO DEMONSTRATE MY POWER

The Nissan Armada and the Mitsubishi Montero are SUVs with needlessly flared wheel wells. The flares don't do anything functional—they only make a big car look bigger and more imposing. Of course, that *is* functional, since the function of the car itself is to appear big. As we saw earlier, that's the reason people buy an SUV in the first place! The cars are muscle-bound, with undulating waves of sheet metal surrounding the tires, making it clear to anyone who drives by that this car is not going to take anything from anyone.

Which is why the bean counters at *Consumer Reports* are dead wrong. The flaring isn't needless at all. A smart marketer in the design department understands that telling a story through the design of the sheet metal is an incredibly cheap way to sell a very expensive car.

Does it make the SUV work better? Well, if your goal is to drive from here to Cleveland, no SUV is going to offer you the best solution. But if your goal is to feel powerful and demonstrate that power to other people, this SUV does exactly what it's supposed to do. It gives you a story you can believe, a lie you can tell yourself every time you see the car.

JACKSON DINER

It's easy to understand the ubiquity of the product-adoption life cycle with a quick look at the Jackson Diner Indian restaurant in Queens, New York. The idea of different people with different worldviews doesn't only apply to technology.

More than a decade ago, chowhound Jim Leff discovered a dumpy little Indian restaurant called the Jackson Diner. He raved about it to his fellow food-obsessed friends and wrote about it in an obscure restaurant guide he published. (Find out more at www.chowhound.com.) The brave and the intrepid rushed out and were delighted with the food, but the diner never got particularly crowded. All the nonfoodies ignored the message because it didn't show up on their radar—the idea of going out for dinner in that neighborhood didn't match up with the prevailing worldview. The Jackson Diner was on the fringes.

Then an actuary named Doron Scharf sent a rave review to the *Zagat Survey* restaurant guide. So did dozens of other foodies. As a result, *Zagat* gave the Jackson Diner a great score, ranking it near the top of their Indian restaurants in New York City.

Within a year, consumers with a worldview that included eating out quite often (that's what makes them loyal *Zagat* readers) were coming to the restaurant. It was a good story ("it's all the way out in Queens . . . only the insiders know about it!") and now it was safe because *Zagat* had recommended it.

Three or four years later, the Jackson Diner has gone downhill. Now it's no better than other Indian restaurants, and in fact in many ways it's worse. The foodies have all left. Management realizes that they don't have to try quite as hard, so they don't.

The irony? It's more crowded now than ever before. People with a mainstream worldview—folks who only want to eat in a restaurant that everyone already goes to—are filling the tables every night. It doesn't matter at all to them that the food isn't good anymore. What matters is that they have a story—"My friend Bob has been going there for years, and the *Times* wrote about it a little while ago"—that makes the Jackson Diner an eclectic but safe dining choice.

That's why the most crowded restaurants are usually not as good as they used to be. As they move through the curve, the success of the restaurant isn't related to how good the food is now. It's related to how good the story is.

THE STORYTELLERS AT AVALON

I'm sitting here looking at a bottle of Avalon Organic Botanicals Therapeutic Rosemary Glycerin Soap featuring 70 percent certified organic ingredients.

This soap (about four ounces in a pump-top green plastic bottle) costs approximately thirty times as much per wash as generic bar soap.

Is it worth thirty times as much? Does it get me thirty times as clean? Does soap really need to be organic? Of course not. And yet I've found a bottle of this soap in the guest bathrooms of at least three different friends' houses.

The Avalon experience begins in the store. It feels good to pick up the bottle. It feels good to know you can afford a luxury like this. It feels good to tell yourself a story about organic fields of rosemary. It's a nice lie to believe that you're giving something back to the planet by supporting this friendly little company.

Using the soap itself is nothing but a reminder of the way you felt (good) when you told yourself a story while buying the soap in the first place. Ready for this? The product is nothing but a souvenir of your trip to the store—and a reminder of the way you felt when you bought it.

Avalon works for the same reason that it's so hard to pawn your engagement ring. It's not the ring—it's the memories. Hand soap as jewelry.

CREATING FOX NEWS

The news on television isn't "true." It can't be. There's too much to say, too many points of view, too many stories to cover. Television can never deliver all of the facts and every point of view. The best a television journalist can hope to do is combine the crowd-pleasing, ad-selling stories on fires and crime with the insightful but less popular stories on world events. And, we hope, to do it without an obvious bias.

Fox News, founded in 1996 by Rupert Murdoch and Roger Ailes, took a different approach. Fox knows that bias exists in any news organization and decided to use this unavoidable problem to frame the news in a way that matched the worldview of their target audience.

What worldviews does this audience share?

- a desire for a consistent story
- a point of view that emphasizes personal responsibility, conservative ethics and Republican politics

- the appearance of fairness, as opposed to being pandered to

That's the way Fox News decided to establish its bias, the way it chose to frame its story. Instead of its being a random mix of individual biases, Fox News chose to tell a coherent story, a lie that its viewers can choose to believe.

Let's start with their slogan, "Fair and Balanced." While one could argue whether their news is fair and balanced, the slogan itself is brilliant. It flatters the audience, reminds them that they are not a tiny minority and reinforces a message that their worldview is valid and appropriate. "News for Conservatives" is precisely the wrong message. Subtlety makes the story work. By acting as though they represent the majority opinion, they frame their story in a way that this audience understands.

Slogans matter, especially here. The worldview of the Fox News audience was that they were disrespected by the established media. Suddenly this audience was watching a network that broadcast news that they agreed with. And they were told that they were the mainstream and that the news that they were hearing was fair and balanced. It made the story irresistible.

Every day Fox management sends a memo to all the writers, producers and on-air talent. The memo outlines the talking points for the day. In other words, it's the story they intend to tell. By managing the news to fit the story (as opposed to the other way around) Fox develops a point of view; it tells a story that viewers are happy to believe. It gives the viewers a lie to tell themselves and, just as important, to share.

By providing a consistent, easy-to-talk-about message, Fox News is telling a story that matches the worldview of their audience—and is easy for that audience to spread. While you can argue about their politics, it is impossible to argue with their success. Roger Ailes understands that he is in the storytelling business and has used that insight to build a multibillion-dollar business.

None of this would matter if Fox News didn't also enjoy climbing ratings. Why does their viewership go up? Because, armed with the lie they believe in, Fox News viewers have an easy time of converting their friends. Fox News is a purple cow, a remarkable phenomenon that's compelling to talk about. As a result, people who would never have chosen Fox News five years ago now watch it regularly. Not because they were persuaded with advertising. Because they were persuaded by their friends and neighbors.

IS A RESTAURANT ABOUT EATING?

Here's a review of a new Thai restaurant that ran in *New York* magazine, "The dining room is centered, more or less, on a limpid reflecting pool, floating with lit candles and water lilies that the wait staff keeps pushing back and forth, possibly to give the impression that we're all drifting down the Chao Phraya River in Bangkok, on some grand royal barge."

Oh. I thought we were having pad thai.

Of course we're not. We're here to be told a story. If that story is authentic and touching and matches our worldview of what we sought, maybe, just maybe, we'll tell our friends.

GETTING SATELLITE RADIO TO SELL

So far, Sirius Satellite Radio has spent more than a hundred million dollars building a nationwide service that delivers radio to cars with an appropriate receiver. Now that the technology is working and the players are available, it's marketing's job to get people to sign up. Sirius has devoted at least as much to signing up new customers as they've spent on building the network.

A traditional marketer would use benefit-based advertising to get the word out. He might target car magazines or audio magazines. Consider these facts about Sirius:

- It works the same anywhere in the country.
- It offers more than one hundred channels.

- There are stations for every genre of music.
- The quality of the broadcast is very good and rarely varies.
- It costs $10 a month.
- The tuner shows you the name of the song.
- You need a special receiver to hear Sirius's broadcasts.

The marketing department at Sirius has to make choices. The facts listed above are far too complex to explain in their entirety. And even if the head of marketing tried, very few people would take the time to hear the facts Sirius was trying to send. They'd ignore the advertising and go on with their lives.

Sirius needs to tell a story. It could be a story about quality and nationwide coverage. The problem? Very few people (mainly truckers) have a worldview that includes the problem "My radio reception is spotty and I want to hear the same songs all over the country." In fact, most people are in the opposite camp: "I don't have a radio problem." If you're walking around believing that you don't have a radio problem, then the greatest radio solution in the world isn't going to show up on your radar. It's invisible.

Even the name is a problem. Sirius Satellite Radio. It implies that this is mysterious, technologically *better* radio. But if I don't believe that my current radio solution is inferior, I'm not going to tell myself a lie about how it could be better.

Sirius could jump through hoops to try to lower the price (I can hear the sales guys now, "The price is too high!"). The price isn't the problem. The problem is that the story doesn't address the needs of the audience, and until it does, no price is low enough. How much would you pay for an anvil? A dollar? What if it was a really nice anvil? A dollar is still too much if you don't believe the story of what the product can do for you.

What about variety? Sirius could try to tell a story about hundreds of different kinds of broadcasts, all the time, every day—without commercials! Alas, the same snag occurs. Most of us don't have the worldview that there isn't enough variety on the radio. It's certainly not a bad enough problem to pay to solve.

So what should Sirius do?

Get Howard Stern.

Not everyone wants to hear Howard Stern. Plenty of people don't even like him. But those who do are open to hear how they can *keep* getting Howard. By taking Howard off real radio and moving him to Sirius, the company has *broken* radio for millions of people. Radio without Howard is inferior to what it was. It needs to be fixed. Sirius can tell me a story of how they can fix it for only $10 a month. The extra stations, the reception, all the gimmicks don't matter. In fact, Sirius shouldn't say a word about the extra features to the Howard Stern people. What matters is that Sirius now has a chance to tell a story to people who want to hear it and to people who will believe it.

Over time the millions of Howard Stern fans who sign up for Sirius will discover the features and some of them may even be compelling enough to tell a story about. And that story will spread.

GETTING PEOPLE TO TRAVEL

The UK travel firm Lunn Poly uses tiny electric dispensers to send wafts of coconut scent through their retail travel agency offices. The smell "has an immediate reaction with customers because it reminded them of suntan lotion and tropical places."

Nobody needs a trip to the Greek Isles. But the things that make us want one are subtle indeed. If travel agencies spent more time with coconut oil and less time finding lower prices on their terminals, they wouldn't be under as much threat from the likes of Travelocity. They need to deliver a personalized experience that you can't get sitting at your keyboard.

THE END OF THE JEWELRY STORE?

Mark Vadon runs bluenile.com, a site designed to suck the profit out of the jewelry business. He's doing that by substituting one story for another. "We want to be the

Tiffany for the next generation," he says. He's already succeeding. Last year, Blue Nile sold more engagement rings than Tiffany & Co.

It's easy to misunderstand his success if you focus on the fact that he sells identical jewelry for half the price of the gems in the famous blue box. **But if cheap is what you want, you can buy cheap cheaper somewhere else. Cheap is not marketing.** Blue Nile is not about cheap. Mark understands that he can always be undersold.

Talking about diamonds, he says, "You learn to appreciate them—where they came from, who cut them. Every one of these has a story."

Blue Nile sold $154 million worth of diamonds last year because, like Tiffany, they tell a story that the buyer believes. Part of that story is about quality, part of it is about being smarter than the poor shmo who gets bullied into buying at Tiffany.

The Blue Nile story is aimed right at guys (the ones who buy engagement rings). The story is framed perfectly for their worldview. That story says, "You're smart enough to buy the right diamond at the right price." Tiffany can't tell that story and neither can the cheapest guys. Women hate the Blue Nile story because it points out that Tiffany is a fraud, selling a blue box for thousands of dollars. Men love it for precisely the same reason.

Is Blue Nile selling a commodity? No. A commodity is

something we need, not want. Nobody needs a diamond. The ironic thing is that jewelry stores that feel they must compete on price are the ones that are creating the end of their industry.

Jonathan Bridge, who runs the Ben Bridge Jewelry chain, says, "We try not to sell diamonds as commodities." The only way to do that is to stop focusing on things like carats and start telling stories instead. In Bridge's words, "Every diamond is different. There's a certain amount of romance in that."

PEOPLE WITH NAPSTER ARE A BAND'S BEST CUSTOMERS

The record industry is, on the whole, obtuse and reactionary and shortsighted, but they also don't pay a lot of attention to worldview.

What sort of person uses (the original) Napster or Limewire or other P2P services? The knee-jerk analysis done by those at the Recording Industries Association is to say, "People who don't want to pay for music." The real answer is, "People with a worldview that says that music (especially new music) is important to them."

Well, that sounds a lot like the worldview of a typical record buyer and concertgoer, doesn't it? Wilco gets this. Wilco is a hugely successful rock band that released their latest album, in its entirety, online for free.

Tim Manners reported that Wilco's Jeff Tweedy explained his view of the nexus of piracy and marketing as this: "A piece of art is not a loaf of bread. When someone steals a loaf of bread from the store, that's it. The loaf of bread is gone. When someone downloads a piece of music, it's only data until the listener puts that music back together with their own ears, their mind, their subjective experience. How they perceive your work changes your work. Treating your audience like thieves is absurd. Anyone who chooses to listen to our music is a collaborator."

Tweedy is telling a story to people who want to hear it, and that story is easy for them to believe. The lie spreads from user to user and pretty soon, instead of being one of five thousand bands trying to get the attention of this very focused group, Wilco is one of a handful. By making the shortlist, Tweedy and Co. end up selling far more albums than they would have if they had insisted that this huge cohort was lying thieves.

THE GOODYEAR BLIMP

If you want to see a shining example of old media, television-industrial-complex thinking, look no further than the Goodyear blimp. By trading overhead camera shots for featured spots on sports broadcasts, Goodyear has made the blimp world famous.

So what? It doesn't sell tires.

Just because everyone knows your name doesn't mean everyone knows your story. They don't believe the lie because there isn't one. All there is, is the blimp and the name.

Michelin has a brand that tells a story (safety). They have a story and people feel good when they buy Michelin tires. Goodyear, on the other hand, gets nothing more out of the blimp than some name recognition and good seats for the CEO at the Super Bowl.

BONUS PART 2: ADVANCED RIFFS

FERTILITY

Different audiences act differently. *Organic Style* readers are nearly twice as likely to have a college education, and more than half recommend products that they have read about in the magazine. The important difference is not in the financial demographics or even the spending levels of the magazine's readership. The difference is in the worldview. Readers of *Organic Style* have friends who are willing to listen to a new story.

The leverage in choosing one segment of the population over another really kicks in when you consider the impact of word of mouth. Music labels correctly focus on college kids, because they're likely to play their music for others and spread the word. An ideavirus can rip through a community on a college campus far faster than it can through a New York apartment building of the same size.

People are not the same. Some people talk, others don't. And quite often, people with similar proclivities join together into populations. College students have more friends and talk with one another more than residents of nursing homes, for example.

Remember, the marketer tells a story. The consumer believes it and it becomes a lie. And that lie can spread from person to person. Then and only then is the marketer going to succeed and will sales grow. Identifying segments that are more likely to embrace this process is an essential first step in telling your story.

Here's a trivial example that makes the point crystal clear. Changethis.com offered free e-book manifestos by well-known authors. Changethis tracked every download and every document that was forwarded through the system. Guy Kawasaki's *Art of the Start* was excerpted by changethis, and the passalong rate through our servers was about 4.5 percent—almost 5 percent of the people downloading this excerpt went ahead and sent it to at least one friend. Tom Peters did a piece on off-shoring, and his passalong rate was 2 percent. Dave Balter, hardly as well known as these two authors, did a piece on buzz and marketing and his was an astonishing 8 percent. This means that Dave's piece, which was downloaded as often as Guy's and Tom's, was 400 percent more likely than Tom's to be shared by one person to another. That's a huge difference.

Even more startling were the results for the piece by Amnesty International about capital punishment. It had a passalong rate of zero.

The lesson? You get to pick the audience you talk to. Dave's audience was aggressive about sharing (sneezing) ideas. Amnesty International's had a different worldview. If you choose an infertile one, you shouldn't be the least surprised to discover that your idea doesn't spread.

WORLDVIEWS CHANGE

What happens to you when you get admitted to medical school?

It turns out that your biases and expectations change a great deal. RBC is the seventh largest bank in North America. They did some research and discovered that they had about 1 percent market share among students in medical and dental schools.

Then they told a story. They told a story exclusively to this group, a story that combined many different elements of the bank and was framed to match the new worldview of this elite group. Here are tens of thousands of young adults who have recently had their outlook on the future radically changed, and they are eager to hear a story about how they can make that future work for them.

Within a few years, RBC's market share went up to

27 percent. According to Richard McLaughlin at RBC, the cost of the program was "a rounding error." He also expects that RBC can grow its market share to as much as 50 percent.

Obviously this is quite a fertile group—at least in the moment they are transitioning from one worldview to another. The hard part isn't selling to them—it was identifying the right group and telling them the right story. You can't change a person's worldview easily, but you can take advantage of the opportunity that presents itself when the world changes it for them.

THE COMPLEX LIFE OF SIMPLE THINGS

Not only do worldviews change, but sometimes the way we feel about a product or service changes over time. Walking through the Albright-Knox Art Gallery in Buffalo, New York, last week, I saw paintings I remembered from my childhood—and felt very differently about them now. The nostalgia overtook whatever I had experienced then. The art meant something different, not because the art had changed, but because I had.

Some professional photographers still use film cameras for catalog work, even though digital is cheaper, faster and more efficient. The reason has nothing to do with the camera and everything to do with the way the camera makes the photographer feel. Over time the film camera ceased to be just a tool and became part of the way that photographer viewed herself and her work. It's not as easy to change a person's worldview as it is to change the technology.

Technologists have discovered that early adopters are likely to fall in hate with a product just as fast as they fell in love with it. If your worldview is to adore the new, then that familiar device you bought a month or two ago is going to have to go, isn't it?

This is one reason why some businesses grow and then stabilize. The corner bar is better when you're a regular—so the regulars stay, while newcomers, the engine of growth, are intimidated and don't even bother coming in. It's not just a place to get a drink—it's a complicated statement about who you are right now.

Nothing is static. Nothing stays the way it was. And everything you build or design or market is going to change the marketplace.

OLD STORIES

When you think about cotton, words like natural, cool, soft and healthy come to mind. That's because you've been telling yourself a story about cotton for a long time, a story that has been encouraged by advertising done by the cotton industry for decades.

It turns out that cotton is a disaster. More toxic pesticides are used to grow cotton than almost any other agricultural product. The cotton industry receives more federal subsidies than any other crop, and it is an amazingly concentrated industry: 80 percent of the money handed out by the government goes to just 10 percent of the growers. Cotton creates far more environmental and social side effects than almost any crop grown. At the same time, high-tech fabrics are lighter, cooler, easier to care for and far less damaging to the environment.

So why haven't we all switched?

Because old stories die hard. As we saw in the examples of Coke and recycling, people don't like changing their minds. It'll be another generation before consumers realize how much damage cotton is doing and start coming to their own conclusions. That's an important lesson for people who work in public policy, but it's a useful insight for someone with a new idea to market: hook it up to an old story.

EXPLAINING FAILURE

If you've worked for months or years and then launched a product or service without success, I'm sure you've been frustrated. I sure have. The worst part is that there doesn't seem to be a straightforward explanation as to why you failed. Sure, it could be a flaw in the product itself or the pricing or even the packaging, but more likely than not, the failure goes unexplained.

Once you look at the world through the lens of the worldview, though, things start to make more sense.

There are four reasons why your new release failed:

1. No one noticed it.
2. People noticed it but decided they didn't want to try it.
3. People tried it but decided not to keep using it.
4. People liked it but didn't tell their friends.

Obvious? Sure. If none of these things went wrong, of course you'd have a success on your hands. Understanding *why* your product failed can give you an insight for next time.

I want to argue that all four of these failures are not your fault. At least they are not the fault of the traditional marketing inputs. Few products fail because they don't work as designed—if they were that bad, they wouldn't be shipped. I believe that most of the seeds of failure are planted long before your product is even manufactured. Marketing starts before the factory is involved. If you choose the wrong story or frame it the wrong way, you lose.

If the worldview of a targeted consumer doesn't permit the story you're telling to resonate, your story fails.

The only recourse is to change that consumer's world-view, and that's almost impossible.

THE FOUR FAILURES

Why didn't anyone notice it? Because they weren't looking. They weren't looking because there's too much to look at and not enough time to take it all in, so our default setting is to ignore everything. We walk a supermarket or a tradeshow or skim a stack of résumés and we actually notice very little.

Most of us have a very simple default frame: if it's not remarkable or exceptional, ignore it. If someone tries to sell you something, decline.

Making something a little better doesn't help you because people won't bother noticing it. (The population isn't monolithic, though, so it's likely that *some* people will bother noticing it. Which leads to the second problem . . .)

Why didn't those who noticed it try it? In most markets, for most products, the frame often carried around says "I'm just looking." Even when we haul ourselves all the way to the mall, that's the answer we give to a prodding salesperson. It's also the way we surf the net—rarely clicking on anything, rarely staying on a Web site for long.

There are segments of the population that are dying to try something. Photography nuts who actively seek out a better lens. Shoe fetishists who will wait in line for a limited edition pair of Nikes. Those are the groups you need to seek out with your story—at least at first.

Why didn't they become loyal customers? While those early adopters (who have a bias to try the new stuff) may have tried it, it doesn't fit their modus operandi to come back for more. The very same bias that pushed them to try your product is pushing them to try someone else's tomorrow.

New products grow when they can peel off a few early adopters and persuade them that they have found the answer to their prayers. This only works when they tell their friends, though.

Why didn't they tell their friends? Why are voters uncomfortable recommending a political candidate to a stranger? To insist that their friends give money to a favorite charity? To talk with a coworker about a new lingerie store?

Why is it so easy to rave about a restaurant or a new CD but not about a massage therapist or the clever way one can save money by buying a casket a few decades early?

Same answer. Worldview. Long before a marketer showed up and asked (insisted, actually) that a consumer forward some note to all her friends, she figured out her comfort level. A goofy Internet video is fine for some people, but you feel really weird talking about gun control. That may not be an intentional delineation on your part, but it's a fact the marketer has to deal with.

Why do certain things grow so fast on the Internet (things like HotMail and Napster and eBay) while others lie there gathering dust? Because of consumer bias about what people feel comfortable sharing—and not sharing. You can whine about this or you can find a category that's more likely to become an ideavirus and tie it into your frame.

THE KEY ADDITION TO PURPLE COW THINKING

In *Purple Cow* and *Free Prize Inside!*, I riffed with you about how to make ideas spread. The essence of that message is that remarkable ideas are going to get re-marked upon—that's how you grow.

You've probably figured out that those books are about the story you tell to *other* people. But before you can tell a story to someone else, you've got to tell one to yourself. The lie a consumer tells himself is the nucleus at the center of any successful marketing effort.

As I write this, I'm looking at a fascinating paper pyramid, two inches tall, subtle yellow stripes printed on beautiful quality linen paper. As I gently unfold the pyramid, a teabag encased in silk falls out. This is tea as a sensual design event, not just a beverage.

Am I likely to rush out and tell everyone I know to go buy a case of Tea Forte ginger lemon herbal tea? Of course not. This tea is not a purple cow. But it is telling a great story—to me.

I get to lie to myself when I make a cup of this tea. I get to promise myself an indulgence, I get to pretend I'm nurturing my inner soul when all I'm really doing is drinking a thirty-cent cup of tea.

By keying into my worldview and making it easy for me to lie to myself, Tea Forte hasn't made a tea for everyone. But Lipton and Tetley already win at the game of making tea for everyone. What Tea Forte has successfully done is create an experience that fills my needs, not my wants. The million-dollar question is whether those who share my worldview are a fertile enough audience to turn this into a real business.

SOME PROBLEMS ARE HARD

Sometimes the prevailing worldview misaligns with the solutions you have to offer and your needs for return and growth.

The new marketing dynamic puts far more pressure on your product design and development people. It makes it much harder to market an ordinary accounting firm or summer camp. My hope is that you will stop relying on marketing as a crutch. If changing your story (and your offering) is the best way to get your message to spread, then that's what you should do instead of whining about how hard it is to get your message out.

GOOGLE ADWORDS AND FINDING THE RIGHT WORLDVIEW

Too many marketers want to find the mass market. Too often the first question is "What's your circulation?" *Good Housekeeping* sells ads for a lot of money because they reach so many moms.

Google adwords are shaking things up because they offer precisely the opposite benefit.

A Google search on "kidney disease" brings up an ad for Dr. Joshua Schwimmer, a nephrology specialist in New York. Dr. Schwimmer can now talk quite confidently to whoever has clicked on his link and visited his page, because he knows their worldview precisely.

The new media proliferating on the Web (blogs and so on) lets you experiment with stories aimed precisely at people who want to hear them. When blogger Joshua Micah Marshall featured tiny ads for unknown congressional candidates in 2004, he helped them raise hundreds of thousands of dollars. Why? Because readers of his blog share a worldview and by framing the ads (and the story) correctly, his advertisers made a connection with people who wanted to hear the story.

OXYMORONS

The words and images you use to tell a story are powerful tools. When those words or images conflict, you've created an oxymoron. Jumbo shrimp and military intelligence are the clichés, but there are countless success stories that were built around oxymorons. Take "compassionate convervatism." By framing a statement around a worldview—and then deliberately confounding expectations—it's easy to tell a story.

Some oxymorons create a conflict that people can't embrace. So they ignore it. A thrift pharmacy selling stale and spoiled drugs, for example, isn't going to fly. Others, though, are challenging enough to the status quo to create a story that some people can't resist investigating.

"Socially conscious investing" won't appeal to everyone. But by connecting two ideas that appear to be in conflict, it's possible to tell a story that many will choose to listen to. Especially if it turns out that the investments are both profitable *and* socially conscious—the story has to be authentic, not just interesting.

The best reason to create an oxymoron is that it may help you address a small, previously unaddressed group that actually *wants* both. That's what happened with the fast-growing adventure cruise lines, and what Starbucks discovered with the Soy Decaf Latte.

"Physical therapy" is an accurate name for the treatment some doctors prescribe to patients with joint problems. Even though physical therapy has a very high success rate (with virtually no complications and a low cost to the patient and the insurance company), it is underprescribed. Why? Because many patients have a worldview that they want to get better fast—with a real doctor.

What if it was called nonsurgical treatment or painless surgery instead?

FRIEND OR FAUX?

Eldon Beck is building a one-hundred-year-old French village in the Alps. He's starting from scratch, and he's doing it for Intrawest, the folks who own ski resorts like Whistler.

Beck's insight is that a new ski resort shouldn't be new. It should have corners that hang out in funny ways and buildings that don't match. Even if it costs more to do it that way.

Intrawest doesn't plan on just hiring hourly workers to staff this village. Instead, they're casting people the way you might cast actors to fill roles. They understand that there's not a lot they can do to make a ski mountain more efficient or appealing, but they can certainly increase the amount of time and money you spend in the village (Intrawest has doubled that figure in the last ten years). Retail anthropologists know that they can only do this by telling a story.

Intrawest does this with single-minded intent. They run a pub in Mount Tremblant where the partying gets so boisterous that patrons often end up dancing on the bar. It turns out that this isn't an accident. Joanne Maislin, an Intrawest planner, made the bar low enough to easily climb on, and put a metal railing on the ceiling so that inebriated patrons will have something to hold on to while they make fools of themselves. It's subtle, because it wouldn't work if it wasn't ("Please dance here" is not going to cut it). The end result is that patrons go back to work a week later talking about what a blast they had—there were even people dancing on the bars!

PROTECT ME

Unfortunately, a common worldview is to be afraid.

There are plenty of things to be afraid of. A broken dishwasher out of warranty. Anthrax. Allergies. Getting trapped inside of your car. The flu. Even sounding dumb at a cocktail party.

While these fears are wildly different, they represent the very same reflex. If your worldview is about protecting yourself or your family, you'll respond extremely well to an offer that's framed in terms of your fear. No, this won't appeal to everyone in a given marketplace. But those grappling with fear are unlikely to respond to anything else.

Last year some people were paralyzed with fear about shark attacks in the Atlantic Ocean. Yet almost no one was mauled, never mind killed. The story was featured in the news and discussed on the beach, but it was only that, a story. It was part of the worldview that many people carried with them. In fact, you are 250 times more likely to be killed by a deer (in a car crash) than by a shark—and there were more gerbil attacks reported in New York in one year than shark bites in Florida. The facts, of course, are completely irrelevant. What matters is what sort of story we're open to hearing.

Every day people are afraid to get on airplanes, even though they are far safer than the car we take to get to the airport. Fear isn't rational. That's what makes it fear, not common sense.

ARE YOU MARKETING A CAMEL?

The Acumen Fund is one of the most extraordinary nonprofit organizations operating today. It is working hard to enable the world's poorest people to become active participants in the world marketplace as consumers, entrepreneurs and employees.

The challenge is not in the facts. The facts are terrific. The challenge is the story.

Jacqueline Novogratz, the CEO of Acumen, envisions an organization that will take the best of the nonprofit world and blend it with the best elements of capitalism. She's trying to help the poor in Africa, Pakistan and Egypt to succeed without being seen as victims. Her model is to raise a fund (she already has $20 million) and use it to invest in locally run companies that offer a product that the poor can afford. Companies selling these items actually raise the standard of living for their customers.

For example, A to Z markets mosquito-repellent window shades in Tanzania. For about $6, a family can be malaria free for five years. The cost of frequent quinine injections (not to mention the risk of death) is far higher than the cost of an A to Z net. A to Z makes a profit, dozens of Africans get good jobs in manufacturing and sales, the villagers save money and Acumen gets a return on its investment.

And that's the problem.

Acumen isn't set up as a traditional NGO, giving charity to people in need. Jacqueline believes that this is a counterproductive, inefficient dead end. Instead, Acumen takes a cut in the companies it invests in, or earns interest on the loans they make to companies.

The grant makers, government agencies and foundations have a worldview that's based on generations of experience. They believe that what they do has value and they're not inclined to believe a story that begins with

"Traditional philanthropy doesn't help the poor very well."

On the other hand, the investment banks, wealthy individuals and hedge funds that are used to making returns on their money have a worldview that says: "We don't care particularly what we invest in. We need our rate of return to beat the industry average by at least x basis points." Acumen's story doesn't register with this audience because they temper their lower-than-market returns with the explanation that they're also doing social good.

If they start with the facts instead of the story, Acumen will be stuck between a rock and a hard place. They have a powerful vision and amazing successes in the works, but the hardest part of their project is here at home—telling the right story to the right people. Big philanthropies hesitate to give because it challenges their model, and big investors hesitate to invest because it doesn't meet their threshold of monetary success.

Traditional marketing thinking would encourage you to just try harder, to hammer again and again on the masses, the big organizations with lots of money to invest.

Acumen found a different path. They are choosing to tell a story to those *dissatisfied* with the traditional stories charities would like them to believe. They are reaching entrepreneurs looking for a different, more efficient philanthropic alternative, as well as foundations that are eager to make a name for themselves by funding organizations with a nontraditional approach to philanthropy.

Imagine some possible oxymorons: Nondonation Philanthropy. Long-term social investments. Return-on-Philanthropy. Social Capital Dividends.

The frustrated donors and the restless investors that Acumen appeals to are clearly at the fringes of their communities. But that's okay. Acumen is crafting a story that these early adopters can tell to their colleagues. They tell their story to the subset of the audience that wants to hear it. At a conference of investors, why not say, "Only 10 percent of you want to hear this story, but that's okay" and then tell the story? By refusing to water down the story, by matching it to the worldview of the audience, Acumen can find those who *want* to believe the story.

Step one is to offer a thrilling story to the people at the edges who want to hear it. Step two is to back that story up with authentic action and proof that it works. Then the bet is that the worldview of "I want to be like my more successful colleagues" will enable the believers to overcome the desire among their peers to take no risk. As Acumen's idea infects these communities, it ought to be able to grow by spreading a new story to people who want to hear it.

ON THE OTHER HAND . . .

Niman Ranch, the leading purveyor of free-range and organic meats, has just announced organically raised, free-range lard.

Hmmm.

They almost nailed the oxymoron. Then, alas, they said, "We'll probably be calling it Saindoux, the French word for lard." Frankie Whitman of Niman said, "We thought 'lard' has too negative a connotation."

Yikes. It seems to me that the negative connotation was the best chance they had to tell a story.

Go ahead, tell me a story.

GOOD STUFF TO READ

FURTHER READING FROM SETH GODIN*

This is the latest book in a series of books I've written about how ideas are invented, transmitted and spread.

For fifty years, advertising (and the prepackaged, one-way stories that make good advertising) drove our economy. Then media exploded. We went from three channels to five hundred, from no Web pages to a billion. At the same time, the number of choices mushroomed. There are more than one hundred brands of

---

*Every nonfiction author ought to include a section like this one. Why? Well, if you've read this far, odds are that your worldview includes a bias in favor of books by this author. By telling you a story about how my books fit together, I make it easier for you to understand the big picture, to spread the ideas and, maybe, to buy some more books.

nationally advertised water. There are dozens of car companies, selling thousands of combinations. Starbucks offers nineteen million different ways to order a beverage, and Oreo cookies come in more than nineteen flavors.

In the face of all this choice and clutter, consumers realized that they have quite a bit of power. So advertising stopped working.

One insight is that marketing with permission works better than spam. In other words, delivering anticipated, personal and relevant ads to the people who want to get them is always more effective than yelling loudly at strangers. *Permission Marketing*, published by Simon & Schuster in 1999, addresses this issue. You can get the first third of the book for free by visiting www.permission.com.

Once an idea is in the hands of people who care about its success, it may be lucky enough to benefit from digitally augmented word of mouth. I call this an ideavirus. Modern ideas spread online and off, and this is faster and more effective than the old-fashioned centralized way of selling. *Unleashing the Ideavirus* is the most successful e-book of all time and you can buy the paperback for about $10 (it's published by Hyperion). Feel free to look for the e-book online as well. It's free.

It's remarkable products that get remarked on. That seems obvious, but it flies in the face of the way most goods and services and business items are created and marketed. Boring is invisible. In *Purple Cow*, published by Portfolio in 2003, I talked about the need to be remarkable.

And finally, the thing that makes something remarkable isn't usually directly related to the original purpose of the product or service. It's the *Free Prize Inside!* (published by Portfolio in 2004), the extra stuff, the stylish bonus, the design or the remarkable service or pricing that makes people talk about it and spread the word.

OTHER BOOKS WORTH READING!*

Crossing the Chasm by Geoffrey Moore

Positioning by Trout and Ries

In Pursuit of Wow! and *The Tom Peters Seminar* by Tom Peters

Blink by Malcolm Gladwell

Selling the Dream by Guy Kawasaki

The Republic of Tea by Bill Rosenzweig and Mel Ziegler

Don't Think of Elephants by George Lakoff

Secrets of Closing the Sale by Zig Ziglar

Why We Buy by Paco Underhill

*Visit www.AllMarketersAreLiars.com to find any of these books (and more) at online stores.

Creating Customer Evangelists by Ben McConnell and Jackie Huba

Emotional Design by Donald Norman

The Moral Economy of the Peasant by James Scott

Creative Company: How St. Luke's Became "the Ad Agency to End All Ad Agencies" by Andy Law

SO, WHAT TO DO NOW?

Do you have a storytelling plan? I believe this needs to become an essential part of any marketing plan or business plan—something that every nonprofit, start-up, big business and politician that intends to succeed must draft. Fill in the blanks and you're on your way.

It starts with a discussion of which group you will tell your story to. The people in a group must share a worldview, a worldview that makes it likely they will sit up and take notice.

Which worldview are you addressing?

If you don't get noticed, you're invisible. You can't tell a story and your marketing ends there and then. The story you'll need to tell in order to get noticed must match the worldview of the people you're telling it to, and it has to be clear and obvious.

Which frame are you using?

How do you frame your story so that people with that worldview will be aware of it, listen to it and believe it?

What's the story that's worth noticing?

Once you've framed it properly, you can tell a subtle story. Use frames to make the stories palatable to people who share a worldview. Tell a story that your audience cares about (and one you can learn to care about!). You only get one chance to tell this story—and it's a story you're going to have to live with. So pick a story that works, not one that your boss likes.

How will you live your story?

Be authentic. Live the story. Making promises you can't keep or selling for the short term instead of the long term is a lousy trade-off. You have a powerful tool—will you use it to make people's lives better?

What hard decisions are you willing to make in order to keep your story real and pure and authentic? Compromise is the enemy of authenticity.

Create mechanisms that allow individuals who believe your story to share it with their friends and colleagues. The way your story will spread is *not* because you directly market to people with a worldview alien to your story. It will spread when one individual interacts with another and uses the power of the personal interaction to spread your story.

> **What are the shortcuts your fans can use to tell the story to their friends? How can you help them frame that story?**

If you can't do this with the product or service you currently offer, *change it!*

> **How can you radically change your product or service so that the story is natural and obvious and easy to tell?**

If you're not growing, the problem is most likely in your product and not your advertising. Have the guts to change it so that it can evolve into what it deserves to be.

> **What's the value of your permission asset?**

Finally, understand that the people with a worldview that gives them a bias to listen to you and to believe you are the most valuable consumers on earth. Get permission from them to follow up, then get to work finding new products for the people who want to buy them.

ACKNOWLEDGMENTS

One last story: I'm very fortunate. As an iconoclast who can be pretty headstrong, I've managed to find a group of insanely smart people who are willing to tell me when I'm wrong. My problem is that I ignore them all too often.

Thanks to Megan Casey, Adrian Zackheim, Will Weisser, Joseph Perez and Allison Sweet at Portfolio. To Lisa DiMona and Karen Watts and Robin Dellabough at Lark. And to Amit Gupta from changethis.

I learned a lot about storytelling in the real world from Sarah Crary Cohen, Carol King, Marcus Jadotte, Dave Balter, Sripraphai Tipmanee, Elizabeth Talerman, Jerry Shereshewsky, Vivian Cheng and Jacqueline Novogratz. Tom Peters even gets his own sentence, because he earned it. This book was inspired by George Lakoff and Malcolm Gladwell.

Red Maxwell, Jonathan Sackner-Bernstein, Jerry Colonna, Tom Cohen, Chris Meyer, Lynn Gordon, David Evenchik, Patti Jo Wilson, Jen Clavier, Charlotte Okie, Richard Primason, Alan Webber, Bill Taylor, Stuart Krichevsky, Michael Cader, Barbara Johnson, Joanne Kates, Marilyn Wishnie, and Drew Dusabout are all-stars (and good friends) who have let me focus on my writing and inspired me to push my work to a different level. Every one of these people is a master storyteller—and an authentic one.

This book is dedicated to Alex, Mo and my dad.
And of course to Helene,
for making the best stories come true.

INDEX

WHAT'S YOUR STORY?

That's what people want to know from you. They want your résumé, your packaging, your candidacy, your ads and your customer service people to tell them a story.

So the challenge you face is now clear. You must have a consistent, authentic story that is framed in terms of the worldview of the person you're telling the story to. Your story must be robust and honest and transparent and you have to be prepared to live it out loud.

Yes, all marketers are liars. But the successful ones are the ones that can honestly tell us a story we want to believe and share.

IF you hope to sell a product or service or candidate or organization that affects the way people feel,

AND IF you hope to get a premium (in revenue or in market share or in votes) for that feeling,

THEN you must refocus your efforts. Concentrate on the story you tell. The story you tell affects the way your audience feels about the product. The story, when you come right down to it, *is* the product.

SOME CONSUMERS will avoid or resist or deny you your story. That's okay. Tell your story to people who want to hear it, who want to believe it, who will tell their friends.

BEFORE you begin to tell your story you have no choice but to live that story. To make it authentic. Every action you take and every signal you send has to be in support of the story.

FINALLY, realize that you are in a powerful position and use that power to do the right thing, to tell the whole truth and to spread ideas worth spreading.